CHASMS of DELIGHT

HOW MIND-EXPANDING DRUGS HELPED TO CHANGE THE WORLD

John Mann

CHASMS of DELIGHT

MEMOIRS
Cirencester

Published by Memoirs

MEMOIRS
PUBLISHING

Memoirs Books

25 Market Place, Cirencester, Gloucestershire, GL7 2NX
info@memoirsbooks.co.uk www.memoirspublishing.com

Copyright ©John Mann, June 2012
First published in England, June 2012
Book jacket design Ray Lipscombe

ISBN 978-1-909020-38-2

Printed in England

CONTENTS

INTRODUCTION

Chapter 1	**FROM ERGOT TO LYSERGIC ACID** - The origins of LSD	Page 1
Chapter 2	**THE MAGIC OF MUSHROOMS** - Psilocybe fungi and the LSD link	Page 7
Chapter 3	**THE POWER OF THE POPPY** - Opium, laudanum and morphine	Page 24
Chapter 4	**A DEADLY INDUSTRY** - Heroin	Page 50
Chapter 5	**COCA AND COLUMBIAN** - Cocaine	Page 66
Chapter 6	**PEACE, POETRY AND POP** - Cannabis, hashish, marijuana	Page 88
Chapter 7	**WITCHCRAFT AND ORGIES** - Belladonna, mandrake and daturas	Page 113
Chapter 8	**HEARTS AND MINDS** - Peyote, mescaline and amphetamines	Page 124
Chapter 9	**DRUNK ON MUSHROOMS** - Fly agaric	Page 139
Chapter 10	**THE GREEN FAIRY** - Absinthe	Page 144

This book is a revised and reorganised version of an earlier
hardback edition published in 2009 by RSC Publishing

For Rosie

My own 60's hippy chick

INTRODUCTION

Timothy Leary's famous exhortation in 1968 to 'turn on, tune in, drop out' has been blamed for persuading the masses to experiment with LSD and other psychedelics, but the truth is that by the 1960s we needed little encouragement to use mind-expanding drugs. Humans had already been experimenting with them for thousands of years. According to Louis Lewin, the German pharmacologist, in his 1924 book entitled Phantastica: *Narcotic and Stimulating Drugs*:

From the first beginning of our knowledge of man, we find him consuming substances of no nutritive value, but taken for the sole purpose of producing for a certain time a feeling of contentment, ease and comfort.

Lewin classified agents capable of changing cerebral function into four main classes:

- Euphorica - sedatives of mental activity which produce a state of physical and mental comfort, eg opium, cocaine and cannabis.

- Phantastica - hallucinating substances, eg mescaline and scopolamine.

- Inebrianta - causing cerebral excitation followed by depression, eg alcohol, chloroform, ether, and benzene.

- Excitanta - mental stimulants, eg caffeine and nicotine.

Lewin could not discuss the mind-expanding properties of heroin or LSD because they had not been discovered, and the large-scale recreational use of many of these drugs was to be a 20th century phenomenon which he could not have anticipated.

There is a continuing fascination with psychedelic, narcotic and euphoriant substances. This book attempts to set out a history of their discovery and use, with an emphasis on the social and anthropological aspects.

In particular, the many colourful characters who have been involved in drug production or use are given prominence. Jerry Garcia of the Grateful Dead is alleged to have said that if you could remember the 60s you weren't actually there – though this comment has also been attributed to several other pop stars of the era. But this is to miss the point about the use of mind-altering drugs, since their effects on the brain are but one of the many areas of interest ascribed to these multifaceted molecules. Their impact on history, politics and social structure are both significant and fascinating, and although most of the substances are tightly controlled, many of them are still widely used. One only has to consider the fact that the war in Afghanistan is probably unwinnable as long as opium is the main crop of that country to appreciate the impact of mind-altering drugs on world affairs.

FROM ERGOTISM TO LYSERGIC ACID

The origins of LSD

To many people the use of recreational drugs dates back to the 1960s, flower power and the Summer of Love. In truth its history is at least a thousand years older.

The active ingredient of LSD (lysergic acid diethylamide) is an ergot alkaloid. This group of molecules is produced by *Claviceps purpurea*, a fungus which under certain conditions invades ears of grain (the purplish-black growth resembles a cock's spur, *ergot* in French). The first historical reference to it dates back to an Assyrian cuneiform tablet from around 600 BC. Humans have been consuming these ergot alkaloids for at least that long, and perhaps since the time of the ancient Mesopotamian empires.

The fertile alluvial lands that lie between the mighty Euphrates and Tigris rivers were the cradle of some of the great early civilizations, including those of the Sumerians, Assyrians and Babylonians. These large and sophisticated nations developed agriculture on a vast scale, with huge annual harvests of wheat and barley and perhaps rye (which was probably first domesticated in what is now Turkey at least 4000 years ago). Thanks to a well-organised peasant workforce, large annual grain surpluses were generated. This allowed people to put down roots, abandoning their former nomadic lifestyle. Suddenly, the concept of spare time appeared. New crafts and written languages flourished.

The dangers of eating ergot-contaminated grain were undoubtedly known in ancient times. Perhaps the earliest description of ergotism can be found in the diaries (the *Annales*) for 857 AD from the convent of Xanten, close to Duisberg on the Lower Rhine in Germany. It was no laughing matter. The Annales report that 'A great plague of swollen blisters consumed the people by a loathsome rot so that their limbs were loosened and fell off before death'. The gangrene that is so graphically depicted here was one of the two types of ergotism, while the other form was most often described as 'convulsive ergotism' and led to so-called 'dancing epidemics.'

The gangrenous, tissue-destroying form of ergotism was apparently commoner west of the Rhine, particularly in France, while the convulsive type – often mistaken for epilepsy – seems to have been more widespread in Germany and Russia. Presumably these differences correspond to the levels of the various ergot alkaloids present in different regional strains of the fungus, and to the way bread was cooked. The major ergot alkaloid is usually ergometrine, which is a potent vasoconstricting agent (constricts blood vessels) and this would be expected to have a significant effect on the blood vessels of the extremities (hence the gangrene). It can also affect the conduction of messages (neurotransmission) in the central nervous system (hence the neurological effects). This effect was certainly recognized and used as early as the 16th century, when the German physician, Adam Lonitzer, described the use of the sclerotia of ergot to stimulate contraction of the uterus and thus 'quicken labour'.

Crude ergot became very popular among the midwives and physicians in much of Europe, despite the severe nausea and vomiting it produced. It was less enthusiastically adopted in America. One physician warned of the serious risk of rupture of the uterus and death of the mother. He even suggested that crude ergot should be renamed *pulvis mortem*. The rising toll of deaths resulting from its use provided the death knell for ergot, at least in America, and by the end of the 19th century it was no longer in use.

One strange occurrence, *La Grande Peur* of 1789, has been blamed on the neurological effects of ergotism. The Great Fear gripped thousands of French peasants for about 18 days at the end of July, engendering riots. Presumably the fall of the Bastille on July 14, triggering the start of the Revolution, and the consequent unrest had something to do with it, but the level of madness across the country seemed so extreme that some other cause has been sought – possibly the ingestion of ergot-contaminated rye. The cold winter and damp spring would certainly have provided ideal growing conditions for the fungus.

A second episode of unexplained behaviour concerns the Salem witchcraft trials of 1692. From December 1691 a number of villagers began to behave in a peculiar way suffering from what were described as 'distempers with disorderly speech' and 'odd postures and convulsive fits', leading to suspicions of witchcraft. At their trial some of the defendants complained of hallucinations and 'crawling sensations in the skin', and all of these symptoms could, in principle, be ascribed to ergotism. Rye was certainly the most successful cereal grown by the New England settlers, and as with *La Grande Peur*, the weather records for 1691 reveal early spring rains followed by a hot and stormy summer, which could have encouraged the growth of ergot. Harvesting and threshing of the crop would have been over by Thanksgiving Day, so the bread baked in December would have been the first to contain ergot if indeed it was present. Whatever the cause of the strange behaviour – and the evidence for ergotism is highly tenuous - by September 1692, twenty villagers had been found guilty of witchcraft and executed.

So far no one imagined there could be anything remotely positive about the consumption of ergot. It was not until the early nineteenth century that pharmacists and chemists began to investigate its chemical constituents. Progress was slow and the first pure component – ergotamine - was not isolated until 1918 by Arthur Stoll at Sandoz in Basel. A second major constituent was isolated in 1935 and called ergometrine. This alkaloid was shown to have a pronounced effect on the uterine muscles, helping to prevent bleeding after giving birth. Since this was a major problem - it still plays a role in the deaths of as many as 150,000 women a year - the introduction of the derivative ergometrine in 1935 was a major lifesaver.

A keen interest in the clinical utility of ergot alkaloids led to further research. Various new derivatives were prepared from the parent alkaloid lysergic acid.

And then, in 1938, came LSD. Stoll and Hofmann at Sandoz Laboratories in Basel, Switzerland, were working on a series of simple amides of lysergic acid, one of which was lysergic acid diethylamide. Initial analysis showed that it had strong oxytocic activity, causing strong uterine contractions with about 70% of the activity of ergometrine.

In the spring of 1943 Albert Hofmann was asked to prepare further quantities of LSD for additional pharmacological studies. On Friday 16th April he was recrystallising a small quantity of the alkaloid when he was overcome by a sense of restlessness and vertigo. In his book *LSD: My Problem Child*, he recalled these effects as written in the report that he submitted to Stoll after the weekend:

I was forced to interrupt my work in the laboratory in the middle of the afternoon and proceed home, being affected by a remarkable restlessness, combined with a slight dizziness. At home I lay down and sank into a not unpleasant intoxicated-like condition, characterized by an extremely stimulated imagination. In a dreamlike state, with eyes closed, I perceived an interrupted stream of fantastic pictures, extraordinary shapes with intense, kaleidoscopic play of colours. After some two hours this condition faded away.

Thinking, not unreasonably, that these effects had been caused by accidental ingestion of LSD, he decided to try a measured dose. On Monday 19th April he deliberately swallowed 0.25 milligram of LSD, a quantity many times higher than the minimum dose required to produce marked behavioural changes. Not surprisingly, the subsequent hallucinogenic experience was very dramatic and he had to ask his laboratory assistant to help him get home.

Due to wartime restrictions on the use of cars, they had to travel by bicycle and by all accounts the journey was terrifying, but at least they reached his home in one piece, which might not have been the case if he had driven. Once home he collapsed on the sofa, with an urgent request to summon the family doctor and fetch milk to use as an antidote. In his book he tells of his experience:

Everything in the room spun around, and the familiar objects and pieces of furniture assumed grotesque, threatening forms. They were in continuous motion, animated, as if driven by an inner restlessness. The lady next door, whom I scarcely recognised, was no longer Mrs R, but rather a malevolent, insidious witch with a coloured mask.

The doctor arrived and after examination reassured him that all his vital signs were normal, though his pupils were extremely dilated. After drinking copious quantities of milk, Hofmann began to relax a little and no longer feared for his life. He even began to enjoy the experience:

Kaleidoscopic, fantastic images surged in on me, alternating, variegated, opening and then closing themselves in circles and spirals, exploding in coloured fountains… Every sound generated a vividly changing image, with its own consistent form and colour.

After several hours he fell into an exhausted sleep. He awoke next morning without any kind of hangover and in fact experienced 'a sensation of well-being' and reported that 'renewed life flowed through me'. Ernst Rothlin, director of the Pharmacology Department at Sandoz, was initially sceptical about Hofmann's report, until two of his colleagues repeated the experiment with smaller doses and reported their own fantastic experiences.

Sandoz could hardly exploit the hallucinogenic properties of LSD, so the company tried very hard to find a therapeutic use for the new drug. They made it freely available to qualified investigators and for a while it looked as if the drug might be useful in the treatment of some psychiatric conditions like schizophrenia, and also as a treatment for alcoholism.

Unfortunately, careful experimentation in the 1950s was often sidelined by sensational magazine articles. After participating in a Canadian LSD study, Sydney Katz wrote one entitled 'My 12 hours as a madman'. Over the years there have been as many reports of adverse reactions to the drug as positive responses, with real dangers for drug takers who experience feelings of omnipotence or invulnerability. Many suicides have resulted from so-called 'LSD psychosis'.

The apparent discovery that chromosomal abnormalities were commonly found in patients after several months of treatment also produced a very negative view of the drug. However, these clinical failures did nothing to dampen the enthusiasm of the emerging hippy culture of the 1960s, which eagerly embraced it.

THE MAGIC OF MUSHROOMS

Psilocybe fungi and the LSD link

Albert Hofmann wasn't through yet. He soon made more discoveries, some of them startling. He brought to light the South American use of seeds of the plant *Rivea corymbosa* (morning glory), which had great significance in Aztec culture.

In the late 1930s, the renowned ethnobotanist Richard Evans Schultes – later to become Director of the Botanical Museum at Harvard University – first suggested that the Aztec magical preparation teonanacatl had been an extract of various species of *Psilocybe* mushrooms. This preparation had been described by Bernardino de Sahagun, a Franciscan friar who accompanied Hernan Cortes on his bloody campaign of conquest of South America in the 16th century. In his report of what he encountered, entitled *Historia General de las Cosas de Nueva Espana*, de Sahagun wrote about a mushroom party:

And they ate the mushrooms with honey – when the mushrooms were taking effect, there was dancing, there was weeping... some saw in a vision that they would die in war, some saw in a vision that they would be devoured by wild beasts... some saw in a vision that they would become rich and wealthy.

Other contemporary writers also refer to mushroom ceremonies. Numerous stone sculptures in the form of mushrooms have been unearthed, many bearing carvings that depict gods or demons, and some of these can be dated as far back as 500 BC. Schultes' assertions were complemented by those of another famous ethnobotanist, R Gordon Wasson, who together with his wife Valentina made many further discoveries concerning the magic mushroom cult associated with *teonanacatl*. In particular, during travels in Mexico in 1955 they managed to track down a village shaman (*curandera*), Eva Mendez, who was prepared to allow them to sample teonanacatl. In a long feature in *Life* magazine in June 1957 he told of his experiences:

The visions came... they emerged from the center of the field of vision, opening up as they came, now rushing, now slowly, at a pace that our will chose. They were in vivid color, always harmonious. They began with art motifs, angular such as might decorate carpets or textiles... then they evolved into palaces with courts, arcades, gardens... resplendent palaces all laid with semiprecious stones. Then I saw a mythological beast driving a regal chariot.

Wasson tried the mushrooms on several occasions, always experiencing similar visions. It was quite clear from his many discussions with the shaman that these ceremonies were a kind of 'holy communion' with the spirits. They were not part of a healing process for sick people but rather a route by which the participants could seek answers to questions through their visions.

Wasson saw this as a fascinating example of pre-Christian practices merging with the new ways of the Catholic Church which had been introduced by the conquistadores and the Franciscan and Benedictine missionaries who accompanied them. Wasson also noted that Eva Mendez had been consuming the mushrooms on a more or less regular basis for 35 years, with no apparent ill effects.

On a subsequent trip, the Wassons were accompanied by a French mushroom expert, Robert Heim, who subsequently managed to cultivate the most important mushroom species, *Psilocybe mexicana*, in his laboratories at the Musée Nationale d'Histoire Naturelle in Paris. Heim sent samples on to Hofmann at the Sandoz laboratories in Basel. Unfazed by his earlier experiences with LSD, Hofmann consumed 32 dried mushrooms (about 2.4 grams) which was reckoned to be a typical dose for the South American Indians, and then recorded his experiences in his laboratory notebook:

Thirty minutes after taking the mushrooms, the exterior world began to undergo a strange transformation. Everything assumed a Mexican character... Whether my eyes were closed or open I saw only Mexican motifs and colours. When the doctor supervising the experiment bent over to check my blood pressure, he was transformed into an Aztec priest and I would not have been astonished if he had drawn an obsidian knife. At the peak of the intoxication, the rush of interior pictures, mostly abstract motifs rapidly changing in shape and colour, reached such an alarming degree that I feared that I would be torn into this whirlpool of form and colour and would dissolve. After about six hours the dream came to an end.

Hofmann went on to isolate and characterize the main psychoactive constituents of *P. mexicana*, which proved to be mainly psilocybin with a little psilocin. Both of these substances are small chemical molecules which have close structural similarity to one of the chemical signalling molecules in the brain - the neurotransmitter 5-HT, also known as serotonin - and block its effects. LSD itself is a much larger molecule, but has buried within its chemical structure a portion that resembles 5-HT, so it too probably interferes with the normal functions of 5-HT.

Since the 5-HT neurotransmitter is implicated in the control of behaviour, mood and sensory responses, it is not surprising that LSD has such a dramatic effect. Psilocybin has only about one per cent of the potency of LSD and use of Psilocybe mushrooms by the hippy culture never achieved the star status of LSD, though these magic mushrooms are still very much part of the way of life of, for example, the Mazatec indians in Mexico.

A further surprise was in store for Hofmann in 1959 when R. Gordon Wasson sent him seeds of *Rivea corymbosa*, a species of morning glory that had been collected in the state of Oaxaca in Mexico. Schultes had already written about this plant in 1941 in his publication for the Botanical Museum of Harvard entitled *A Contribution to our Knowledge of Rivea Corymbosa: the Narcotic Ololiuqui of the Aztecs*. A much earlier description of ololiuqui had been written by Francisco Hernandez , physician to Philip II of Spain, during his travels in South America during the period 1570-75. He described the preparation of ololiuqui and noted:

When the priests wanted to commune with their Gods and receive a message from them... they ate this plant and a thousand visions and satanic hallucinations appeared to them.

To Hofmann's amazement, the major chemical constituents of *Rivea corymbosa* seeds were derivatives of lysergic acid with an uncanny structural resemblance to LSD. In fact these substances subsequently proved to be about 20 times less potent, and were mostly narcotic rather than hallucinogenic. When Hofmann first presented his results at an international Congress on Natural Products in

Sydney in 1960 there was considerable scepticism that similar compounds could be found in a plant and a fungus, since these types of organism belong to completely different kingdoms. None the less Hofmann had now been responsible for establishing the involvement of ergot alkaloids in the cultures of peoples on two continents separated by the vast expanse of the Atlantic Ocean.

These primarily scientific activities caught the imagination of a growing number of psychiatrists, who speculated that consumption of magic mushrooms or LSD might help patients to reveal their innermost problems. One of the prime movers in this area was a young Harvard academic called Timothy Leary.

Leary did more than anyone else to popularize the cult of LSD. Within a few years his enthusiasm for this drug would earn him the opprobrium of much of the US hierarchy, including President Nixon, who (prior to his own impeachment) labelled him 'the most dangerous man in America'.

Leary had completed a PhD in Psychology at the University of California at Berkeley in 1950, and became, in 1955, the Director of Psychiatric Research at the Kaiser Family Foundation Hospital. He even wrote a 518-page textbook entitled *The Interpersonal Diagnosis of Personality*, which received very favourable reviews.

At the end of 1959 he accepted a position as Assistant Professor at the Harvard Center for Personality Research and appeared to be on track for a promising academic career. Until, that is, he spent a vacation with colleagues Richard Alpert, Anthony Russo and other mutual friends in a small Mexican village called Cuernavaca. Evidently the conversation turned to magic mushrooms. They managed to locate a local Indian *curandera*, who sold them a bag of mushrooms which apparently contained psilocybin. The resultant experience changed Leary's life, and he returned to Harvard determined to carry out scientific research in a new research group that he christened the Harvard Psilocybin Research Program. He even persuaded Harvard to fund a project that sought to examine the clinical effects of psilocybin.

Sandoz very kindly agreed to supply the drug, which had been isolated as a result of Hofmann's earlier studies, and Leary and his collaborators now had to plan their experiments carefully, since this was uncharted territory. Well – almost. It was around this time that Aldous Huxley, author of the highly influential *Brave New World* (1932), came to Massachusetts Institute of Technology as a visiting professor. Back in 1953 he had experimented with mescaline from the peyote cactus. This was yet another of the magical Mexican preparations commonly know as peyotl, and one that had been investigated in the clinical setting of the Maudsley Hospital in London during the 1930s. Huxley had written about his experiences with mescaline in his 1954 book *The Doors of Perception*, and it is quite clear from the text that he considered mescaline to be a force for good, since it allowed the user to gain insight into the world around them.

While at MIT, Huxley and Leary spent some time together discussing Leary's proposed research programme. Both apparently had firm views that the correct use of psychedelics could divert humans from warlike and other violent preoccupations. This led Leary to carry out psilocybin experiments not only with students and colleagues at Harvard, but also within prison populations, to see if psychedelics could reduce the level of reoffending once the prisoners were released.

Various pseudo-religious investigations were also carried out at this time to compare the psychedelic experience with those described in the Bible and elsewhere, where people reported having visions and claimed to have experienced 'ecstasy'. Not surprisingly the Church began to take notice of this academic who claimed that a pill could produce experiences hitherto claimed to be achievable only when one came close to God.

But Leary was about to ruffle more feathers. He embarked upon a programme of research that would cause fear and consternation not only in the Church but all the way to the White House.

Leary is reputed to have been introduced to LSD by an Englishman, Michael Hollingshead, an equally colourful character who, it is claimed, obtained a gram of LSD from Sandoz simply by writing to the company on official notepaper from a New York Hospital and claiming that he needed the drug for medical experiments. Whatever the truth of this claim, Hollingshead visited Leary at Harvard and persuaded him to take his first trip with LSD.

Leary quickly became something of an evangelist for LSD. He criss-crossed America giving lectures and talking to influential people, trying to impress on them the ways in which LSD allowed people to explore the realities of their lives by 'reprogramming their brains'. His extended absences from Harvard, not to mention the growing pressure from the parents of students who were alarmed by the bizarre stories of LSD use by their offspring, eventually led to Leary being sacked from his position in 1963. He seems to have been unfazed by this. In any case he was busy setting up his International Foundation for Internal Freedom in Cambridge Massachusetts and a kind of summer school in Mexico for those who wanted to experience the mind-expanding possibilities offered by LSD. However, the centre in Mexico only survived for one summer before being closed by the Mexican police, and Leary and his team were deported. To make matters more difficult for him, the Federal Drug Administration now decided that LSD was too dangerous to be used in a non-clinical setting. Supplies of the drug from Sandoz became highly controlled, and the company stopped manufacturing both LSD and psilocybin in August 1965.

The CIA had also now taken a keen interest in Leary's activities, not least because they had been carrying out their own investigations into the utility of LSD as an incapacitating agent for the battlefield. The actual extent of these activities only came to light during a Senate Enquiry in 1977, which revealed a plethora of covert activities on chemical and biological weapons covered by the codename MK-Ultra. The revelations about experiments on prisoners and mentally-ill patients using LSD were, of course, defended on the grounds of national security during the period of the Cold War with Russia and her allies. Having lost his job and his summer school, Leary had to find a new base for his activities. Once again his luck held, and he was allowed to set up an experimental commune in a 64-room mansion at Millbrook in New York State. This gothic pile was used by the grandchildren of the immensely rich Mellon family, who were persuaded of the benefits of LSD, and it was here and on a later trip to India that Leary formulated his new religion, which he christened the League of Spiritual Discovery. There were just two commandments:

Thou shalt not alter the consciousness of thy fellow man.

Thou shalt not prevent thy fellow man from altering his own consciousness.

The League's manifesto - *we solemnly publish and declare that we are free and independent, and that we are absolved from all allegiance to the United States Government and all governments controlled by the menopausal* – did little to endear Leary to the Government, who viewed him as a subversive. That view was confirmed when he gave his now-famous speech to the huge crowd of around 30,000 attending the 'Human Be-In' held in San Francisco in January 1967. The speech contained his immortal appeal:

The only way out is in – turn on, tune in, drop out! Of High School, junior executive, senior executive. And follow me! The hard way!

Subsequently Leary sought to explain this apparently negative advice. He claimed that 'turn on' implied an activation of the mind through drug use; 'tune in' meant achieving harmonious interaction with the world; and 'drop out' meant detachment from the world. So the exhortation was not at all subversive.

Whatever the true meaning of his words, Leary had an undoubted influence on what became the 1967 'Summer of Love', centred in the Haight Ashbury district of San Francisco and celebrated around the world in an orgy of flowers, music and psychedelic drugs. This outbreak of love and peace caused further alarm and consternation to a government that was fighting (and by now losing) the war in Vietnam, so it was inevitable that Nixon's 'most dangerous man in America' would sooner or later fall foul of the law. It happened on Boxing Day 1968, when Leary was arrested in California allegedly in possession of marijuana. Despite his plea that the drugs had been planted, he was sent for trial.

While awaiting his court appearance he found time to announce his candidacy for the Governorship of California - against Ronald Reagan – and his campaign slogan was COME TOGETHER, JOIN THE PARTY. He also joined John Lennon and Yoko Ono at their well-publicised Montreal Bed-in in June 1969; but such activities were soon to be curtailed. At trial in January 1970 he was found guilty and sentenced to ten years in prison. Initially he was incarcerated in the maximum security prison at Chino in California, and there was talk of a transfer to the notoriously violent prison at Soledad, but Leary was fortunate enough to be given a psychology test that proved he would make a model prisoner, so he was transferred to the low security prison at San Luis Obispo.

What the prison psychologist did not know was that Leary had been responsible, at least in part, for the questions used in the personality test, so he knew all the right answers!

That is where the story should end, but Leary was such a larger-than-life character that it was almost inevitable he would escape. In an escapade that rivaled action seen in the Indiana Jones movies, he escaped from San Luis Obispo prison on the evening of 12th September 1970.

There are claimed to be at least seventeen different versions of the escape story, mostly due to Leary. What seems to have happened is that he escaped by scaling a tree in the prison yard, clambering over the roof of the cell block and descending to freedom via a conveniently-located telegraph pole. His wife Rosemary was waiting for him with a getaway car and with the additional help of the Weathermen – a revolutionary group bent on national disruption – he eventually flew out of New York on a false passport and into exile in Algeria.

At this time Algeria had just emerged from a vicious colonial war of liberation with its French colonial masters, and the Algerian government were well disposed to other liberation groups from around the world, including the American Black Panther movement, whose ambassador in Algeria was the infamous Eldridge Cleaver.

The Learys sought refuge with Cleaver, and since they had brought with them a supply of high-quality LSD, the welcome was initially very warm. However, this warmth was soon compromised by Leary's enthusiasm for talking to the world's press, including *Playboy* and *Rolling Stone*. His claims for the sexually excitant properties of LSD, especially stories about the huge number of female orgasms that could be achieved on one dose, were widely reported. In addition, his outpourings about drug use caused embarrassment for the new revolutionary Islamic government. Soon the Learys were looking for a new place of exile, which they found in Switzerland.

Interestingly, while in Switzerland he made arrangements through his lawyer to have lunch with Albert Hofmann, and the two met in a railway station snack bar in Lausanne. In his book *LSD: my problem child*, Hofmann writes that he told Leary of his personal regret that promising scientific experiments with LSD and psilocybin had been overshadowed by the indiscriminate use of the drugs by the hippy culture. However, he went on to say (somewhat naively) that he was encouraged by Leary's very definite discrimination between the addictive drugs like morphine and heroin and the others (LSD, psilocybin and mescaline) that he felt were a force for good in the world.

Hofmann also expressed concern that Leary was careless of his own safety, and this proved to be the case. In January 1973 Leary's luck ran out when he was arrested on a trip to Afghanistan and repatriated to serve the rest of his sentence. He was subsequently released early on licence in April 1976. The next 20 years were spent writing and giving lectures, though the glamour of LSD had now largely passed, primarily because its sheer potency meant that its effects were unpredictable. Other drugs like marijuana, cocaine and heroin were also much more easily available.

Timothy Leary died in May 1996, and a year later some of his ashes were blasted into space along with those of Gene Roddenberry – creator of Star Trek – and others.

Although it is all too easy to exaggerate Leary's contributions to the history of LSD, the influence of this drug on the pop music of the late 1960s is usually held up as a very tangible example of its 'mind expanding' properties. Compare, for example, the lyrics of most of the tracks of the Beatles' *Sergeant Peppers Lonely Hearts Club Band* - eg *Lucy in the Sky with Diamonds* - or the Beach Boys' *Pet Sounds*, or Bob Dylan's *Highway 61 Revisited* (especially *Desolation Row*), with the words of the songs on their earlier records, and the probable influence of LSD is apparent. John Lennon always claimed that the title *Lucy in the Sky with Diamonds* had nothing to do with LSD, but was inspired by a school painting produced by his young son Julian. Of the four Beatles, Lennon appears to have been most influenced by Leary, who was present at the famous recording session of *Give Peace a Chance*, and appears in the video.

The Beatles always claimed that they first experienced LSD in 1965 when someone 'spiked' their drinks at a party in London. In his definitive biography *Shout*, Philip Norman records Cynthia Lennon's account of their nightmarish journey home, with John crying and banging his head against the car sides and Pattie Boyd (George Harrison's wife) attempting to leave the moving vehicle in order to break windows in Regent Street. None the less Lennon reputedly took hundreds of LSD trips, and this undoubtedly contributed to the growing instability within the Beatles.

Much so-called 'psychedelic art' appeared during the 1960s, but it is now generally accepted that painting while inebriated with LSD was not possible, since the rush of images is too great to be captured on canvas or paper. However, genuine works of psychedelic art could be inspired by the experience once it was at an end. More imaginative stories about the influence of LSD on Francis Crick's discovery (with James Watson) of the DNA double helix and on Bill Gates' early work on computer programs have to be taken with a very large pinch of salt.

The huge interest in LSD in the 1960s and 1970s, its restricted availability from the pharmaceutical suppliers and its relative ease of synthesis led to a large cottage industry involved in making the drug illicitly. One particularly interesting example is worth relating, since it was based almost wholly in the UK. The originator of this clandestine operation was the American Ron Stark, who was a member of the Brotherhood of Eternal Love, one of the many splinter groups that had grown out of the activities in Haight Ashbury. It was this group who were claimed to have funded Leary's escape from prison.

Stark met and persuaded the young English chemistry graduate Richard Kemp to go into production. Kemp had obtained his BSc at the University of Liverpool, and was studying for his PhD when he was persuaded in 1970 to join Stark's illicit laboratory in the suburbs of Paris. Here he is alleged to have been involved in the synthesis of about a kilo of LSD.

Having learned his trade, Kemp then returned to England to live with his partner Christine Bott, whom he had met at university while she was studying medicine. They set up a number of small-scale synthesis operations in various rented flats in and around London and employed the one-time accountant Henry Barclay Todd to turn the synthetic LSD into tablet form (usually in the form of microdots on blotting paper) in a house in Seymour Road in Hampton Wick. These tablets were then passed on to various dealers, many of whom were students at Reading University, and were well placed to service the needs of those attending the various pop festivals in the Thames Valley area.

A further participant, the American author David Solomon, travelled to Germany to buy ergotamine tartrate from the small company Dr Rentschler, and this was then stored in safety deposit boxes in Zurich and Geneva until Kemp collected it for transport back to England.

He and Bott moved into a remote farmhouse at Blaencaron near Tregaron in Wales from around 1975, and another house at nearby Carno was rented for the actual chemical synthesis. The necessary purchases of chemicals and small bits of equipment were made by Todd (under a number of aliases) from British Drug Houses and from Hopkins and Williams.

The paper records of these transactions were to prove vital as evidence in the eventual prosecution. From the initial batch of ergotamine it is claimed that Kemp and Bott made around 1.7 kilos of LSD, which was enough to provide about 8.5 million doses of 200 microgram each. These were sold as small tablets known as 'microdots' and were of exceptional purity. The operation went from strength to strength, and by mid 1976 they were probably supplying about 95% of the UK's needs and about 50% of the worldwide requirements.

Most of the information about these clandestine operations comes from the book *Operation Julie*, written jointly by Dick Lee (the Thames Valley police inspector in charge of the successful investigation) and the journalist Colin Pratt, and from the various TV documentaries that have been made about the operations. Kemp and Bott were only discovered after a series of misfortunes, most notably the impounding of Kemp's car after he was involved in a fatal accident. But even before this, in April 1975, Lee had been suspicious about the amount of LSD being seized at rock festivals in the Thames Valley region, though he was actually investigating the arrival of large amounts of cannabis in VW caravanettes, imported from Morocco into the Reading area. During an undercover operation one of the local cannabis dealers revealed that he could obtain LSD for them, but he disappeared into a hippy commune near Tregaron before the police could extract further information. When he was subsequently tracked down he would not reveal his sources, though by now Scotland Yard's drug squad had passed on to Lee the names of several people they were interested in, which included Kemp and Bott.

Fortunately for the police investigation, the local Welsh police recalled the recent accident involving Kemp's red Range Rover and the forensic team re-examined the vehicle. On this second search some scraps of paper were found which when pieced together revealed the word *hydrazine hydrate*. Someone had enough chemical knowledge to realize that this might be used in the LSD synthesis. In the early days of ergot research, hydrazine had been used to convert the complex ergot alkaloids, including ergotamine, into lysergic acid.

It took almost a year for Lee to persuade his superiors in the Thames Valley Police Force to fund further investigations, but finally in April 1976 the farmhouse at Blaencaron was put under police surveillance in a high-profile investigation code-named Operation Julie (named after a member of the crime squad). Kemp was seen to spend several days at a time in the house at Carno and the rest of the time with Bott at Blaencaron.

In May the police broke into the house at Carno while Kemp was away, and although there was little overt evidence of any major synthetic activities, they found two near-empty drums of methanol and a dead mole in one of the drains. Subsequent examination at the Government forensic laboratory at Aldermaston provided evidence of LSD intoxication in the mole, together with definite evidence of LSD in the drain effluent. This laboratory and its senior chemist – Neville Dunnett –were to have a key role in the analysis of material discovered in Wales, Hampton Wick and elsewhere.

Examination of records of water consumption at the Carno house showed that 500,000 gallons had been consumed over the previous 18 months, which was about ten times the amount consumed by a normal household and would support the existence of an illicit chemical operation.

Just as the investigation seemed to be moving towards a successful conclusion, Kemp abandoned the Carno laboratory and returned full-time to domestic bliss with Christine Bott at Blaencaron. The distribution network was also proving difficult to identify until the police managed to infiltrate a group led by John McDonnell and William Lochhead in the summer of 1976. In a sting operation centred in Wiltshire, the undercover agents managed to buy LSD tablets which were matched to others believed to have originated from the Welsh operation. Then in November, Kemp began to extend the plumbing in a newly rented cottage at Esgairwen about four miles from Lampeter, and this work included a new drain system to lead effluent into a nearby stream. Obviously the synthetic operation was about to restart.

Finally, on March 25th 1977, after a winter of further observation and evidence gathering, the house in Seymour Road was raided. Todd's tableting laboratory was discovered complete with appropriate chemicals, drying trays, some LSD tablets, around 250mg of pure LSD and about £20,000 hidden in packets of Alpen cereal. Todd and several accomplices were arrested in the house.

The next day, the cottages at Esgairwen and Blaencaron were raided and Bott and Kemp were arrested. Under interrogation, Christine Bott revealed the location of some of the LSD that had been produced, together with the existence of a safety deposit box in a Zurich bank. Later excavation under the kitchen floor tiles in the Blaencaron cottage revealed around 1.3 kg of pure LSD, worth about £65 million on the street.

At the subsequent trial seventeen people were found guilty of various offences. Kemp and Todd both received sentences of 13 years, while Bott received one of 9 years and 14 others received sentences ranging from 2-11 years. Although more of the LSD tablets were recovered from caches in woods in Berkshire, most of the money that must have been earned by the participants has never been recovered.

The mode of action of LSD is still poorly understood. Its ability to cause changes to the senses, for example how it allows people to 'hear' colours and 'smell' sounds, is almost impossible to comprehend. It can precipitate flashbacks many weeks after it has been ingested, and there have always been concerns that frequent use could lead to long-term psychosis. What is known is that the main pathway by which it exerts its effects is via interference with the normal functioning of the neurotransmitter 5-HT (serotonin) within the brain. In particular, it competes with serotonin for 5-HT receptors, especially in the hypothalamus and brain stem, though this competition is far from uniform in different parts of the brain.

In May 2008, approval was given for a Swiss study which is now exploring the use of LSD to ameliorate anxiety in terminally-ill cancer patients.

Whatever the future holds for LSD, there is no doubt that discovery of its interactions with the 5-HT system in the brain contributed to other research that led to the discovery of anti-depressants like Prozac and Zoloft, and also to migraine drugs like Imigran. Both of these conditions – depression and migraine – involve disturbances in 5-HT function.

In the UK, LSD is categorized as a Class A drug in the same group as heroin and cocaine, so it is illegal to supply it, buy it or use it. Any of these crimes can attract a prison sentence of up to 10 years. The other ergot alkaloids no longer have widespread use within a clinical setting and thankfully they are only very rarely responsible for outbreaks of ergotism.

Those three larger-than-life characters R. Gordon Wasson, Timothy Leary and Albert Hofmann will be remembered for a long time to come. In an interview with Leary just before he died, he was asked by a reporter what he thought of Nixon's claim that he was the most dangerous man in America. Leary replied: 'Yes it's true – I have America surrounded'. An amusing epitaph for this interesting man. But the final words must be those of Albert Hofmann, who died in May 2008 aged 102:

During the first years after its discovery, LSD brought me the same happiness and gratification that any pharmaceutical chemist would feel on learning that a substance he or she produced might possibly develop into a valuable medicament. The more its use as an inebriant was disseminated, bringing an upsurge in the number of untoward incidents caused by careless, medically unsupervised use, the more LSD became a problem child for me.

CHAPTER THREE

THE POWER OF
THE POPPY

Opium, laudanum and morphine

Yea, slimy things did crawl with legs
Upon the slimy sea.
About, about, in reel and rout
The death fires danced at night;
The water, like witch's oil,
Burnt green, and blue and white.

These lines by the English poet Samuel Taylor Coleridge about the horrors seen by the crew in his *The Rime of the Ancient Mariner* may have been influenced by the effects of opium. While the poem was written before Coleridge became addicted himself, there is little doubt that he wrote it while treating himself with the drug for his dysentery.

Such influences of opium on artistic output greatly postdate its medical uses, which were probably discovered by the Ancient Sumerians as long ago as 3400 BC. Ideograms on stone tablets have revealed the method of collection of crude opium, which involved scoring the unripe seed capsules of the poppy plant with a knife to allow a milky exudate to 'bleed' from the capsule, then returning the next day to scrape off the congealed latex. Often the harvesters would walk though the fields wearing leather aprons, to which the latex adhered.

The exudate was then usually treated with boiling water, in which it dissolved. Impurities were filtered off, then the water evaporated to leave a brown, mobile liquid which dried to leave a thick brown paste of crude opium. These methods have changed surprisingly little over the millennia. Of the numerous species of poppy only *Papaver somniferum* (and to a lesser extent *Papaver setigerum*) contain significant quantities of opium alkaloids, with morphine comprising up to 20% by weight of crude opium (with codeine up to 2.5% and thebaine up to 2%). Although there is ample evidence of seeds of both plants in Neolithic sites, only *Papaver somniferum* was domesticated to provide the plant that we call the opium poppy.

None of the early references to the opium poppy mention recreational use. Right up until mediaeval times there was an almost complete emphasis on medical uses, though these did include mixtures of opium and various poisons (especially hemlock) as agents for euthanasia. It was probably the Ancient Egyptians who first popularised the medical uses of opium. The Ebers papyrus, from about 1500 BC, contains several hundred preparations for the treatment of myriad conditions including hair loss (no likely efficacy) and childhood colic (excellent chance of success). Indeed opium produced in Thebes became famous from around 1300 BC and was exported to numerous countries that bordered the Mediterranean Sea.

The growing importance of opium from around this time is clear from its association with deities in many societies like the Minoan goddess (of narcotics?) depicted with her garland of poppies, the minor deities associated with sleep (Greek - *Hypnos*, Roman - *Somnus*), and death (*Thanatos*) usually shown with poppy wreaths. Most references to other medicinal uses of opium come to us from ancient Greek texts, and Homer's *nepenthe* was probably a mixture of opium and wine. In the *Odyssey* he describes its use as an aid to forgetting the trials and tribulations of the Trojan war:

Helen, daughter of Zeus, poured a drug, nepenthe, into the wine they were drinking which made them forget all evil. Those who drank of the mixture did not shed a tear all day long, even if their mother or father had died, even if a brother or beloved son was killed before their eyes by the weapons of the enemy.

The great Greek physicians like Dioscorides, Theophrastos and Hippocrates all recognised that 'poppy juice' induced sleep and could reduce pain. Later, Greek medicine was the main influence in the Roman Empire. Probably the greatest advocate of opium was the Greek physician Galen (second century AD). He claimed the poppy extract as a panacea which he christened *mithridatium*, and prescribed it for just about every condition from colic and headache (where there was real efficacy) to leprosy and menstrual problems (doubtful). He also made a genuine contribution to the study of the toxicity of opium, and in particular noted the induction of tolerance such that the patient needed to take larger and larger doses in order to have the same effect. He reported that the Emperor Marcus Aurelius used a mixture of opium and honey to help him sleep.

As usual the Romans were not slow to take advantage of new opportunities to dispatch one another, and it is possible that in AD 55 the Emperor Claudius' fourth wife Agrippina poisoned her stepson Britannicus with opium so that her son Nero would have no rival to his claim to become Emperor. If true, this is an early example of the malevolent influence of opium on history. In addition, the Romans were the first to take seriously the recreational possibilities of opium, though there is little reliable record of excesses like those observed later in China.

As with all empires the Roman influence waned, and from around the fourth century the Arabs became the dominant force in the eastern Mediterranean and the Middle East. Their influence on medicine and learning was unrivalled in the region for nearly a thousand years, from 500-1500 AD, and many of their contributions to architecture still provide testimony to this golden age. In their great library in Alexandria they maintained copies of all the great Greek and Roman texts on medicine, thus ensuring that the medical lore of giants like Galen and Dioscorides would survive right up until the present day. In particular, the mammoth five-volume *De Materia Medica of Dioscorides*, written between AD 60 and 78, and the 20 volumes of Galen's *Opera Omnia* (which appeared around AD 170), formed the basis of most prescribing right through to Elizabethan times.

The Arab medical experts embraced opium as a treatment for pain and stomach disorders, and as their empire spread westwards into Spain and eastwards as far as India, they took it with them. In fact they were probably the first to introduce the plant extract into China.

Of the Arab physicians, Abu Bakr Al-Razi or Al Razes (865-923) and Abdallah Ibn Sina or Avicenna (980-1037) were the most influential. The former was both a medical expert and an alchemist who extolled the virtues of opium in anaesthesia, and was also experienced in the science of distillation. Avicenna managed to combine an adventurous lifestyle with a prolific output as an author of philosophical, medical and herbal texts, many of which were still in use centuries later. His *Canon of Medicine* (translated into Latin by Gerardo de Cremona around 1140) was the most influential, and of the 760 drugs mentioned it highlighted the value of opium as a narcotic.

It was this book and the works of Galen that were ceremonially burned in 1526 by that most infamous and splendidly-named of sixteenth century physicians, Philippus Aureolus Theophrastus Bombastus von Hohenheim, usually known as Paracelsus. Paracelsus was born near Zurich in 1493 and after training periods in Switzerland, Germany and Austria, received his doctorate in medicine from the University of Ferrara. After several years of travelling, he was appointed Professor of Medicine in Basel in 1526, promptly vilifying the plant-based drugs of Galen and Avicenna and publicly burning their books. He then embarked on a crusade that emphasised the salts of arsenic, antimony, tin and mercury for treatment of all manner of ailments. He was also not above using magic, necromancy and astrology, and is reputed to have introduced the use of laudanum.

Paracelsus claimed: 'I possess a secret remedy which I call laudanum and which is superior to all other heroic remedies'. That he invented laudanum is almost certainly untrue, but his recipe for this is claimed to have included about 25% of opium mixed in with henbane, amber, musk and various more unusual ingredients including bezoar stone - in reality an accretion from cow's intestines – and crushed unicorn horn, which was probably sea shells. Whatever its actual composition, laudanum became synonymous with the various preparations of opium that were dispensed, most of which later involved dissolution of the poppy extract in wine or purer forms of alcohol.

Another populariser of opium was the Spanish physician Cristobal de Acosta, who produced, in 1582, a treatise on medicines from the East Indies. His work was widely regarded, not least because he recommended opium as an enhancer of sexual performance and particularly extolled its virtues in the prevention of premature ejaculation.

Other famous herbalists enthused about the benefits of opium. John Gerard, undoubtedly the most important Elizabethan advisor on drugs, provided a very apposite description in his *Great Herball* (1597);

It mitigateth all kinde of paines, but it leaveth behind it oftentimes a mischief worse than the disease itselfe.

The greatest populariser of opium was Thomas Sydenham, born (or at least christened) in Wynford Eagle, Dorset in 1624. He received his Bachelor of Medicine from Oxford in 1648, and practised as a physician first in Oxford and later in London. Although he is most often associated with the introduction of the bark of the Cinchona tree (and hence quinine) as a treatment for malaria, which was endemic in many parts of Britain, he was also fulsome in his praise for opium:

Among the remedies which it has pleased the Almighty God to give to man to relieve his sufferings, none is so universal and so efficacious as opium.

In the first volume of his Works, first published in Latin in 1676 (with a translation into English in 1742 by John Swan), Sydenham summarised the utility of opium:

So necessary an instrument is opium in the hand of a skilful man, that medicine would be a cripple without it; and whosoever understands it well, will do more with it alone than he could well hope to do with any single medicine. To know it only as a means of procuring sleep, or of allaying pain, or of checking diarrhoea, is to know it only by halves.

Sydenham's preparations were based upon opium and saffron in the ratio of 2:1, combined with a pinch of cinnamon and cloves (to mask the bitter taste), all dissolved in 'canary wine'.

Sydenham was friendly with several of the soon-to-be famous Oxford crowd, and of these it is recorded that Christopher Wren and Robert Boyle experimented in 1656 with the new technique of injection using a hollow quill. They reported that a dog became extremely stupefied after an injection of a warm solution of opium.

The first major work in English that concentrated on the uses of opium was provided by the Welsh physician John Jones in 1700 in his book *Mysteries of Opium Reveal'd*. He assured his readers that:

It takes away grief, fear, anxieties, peevishness, fretfulness… and causes a great promptitude to venery and erections.

But he did warn of the severe suffering of withdrawal from opium addiction:

Great and even intolerable distresses, anxieties and depressions of spirits which in a few days commonly end in a most miserable death.

One of Thomas Sydenham's pupils, Thomas Dover, invented the very popular Dover's Powder, which comprised opium, liquorice, ipecacuanha (usually an emetic), saltpetre and vitriolated tartar, all to be mixed and taken in white wine. In his youth Dover travelled widely and was for a while a privateer. It is even claimed that in 1709 he was the saviour of Alexander Selkirk, who had been marooned on the island of Juan Fernandez off the coast of Venezuela, later to become the model for Robinson Crusoe. But even the popularity of Dover's powder paled in contrast to 'Godfrey's cordial' (a mixture of opium, spices and treacle in water) which was being sold at the rate of several gallons per week by some pharmacies in the big industrial cities like Manchester and Nottingham during the 18th and 19th centuries. Other popular preparations included Mrs Winslow's Soothing Syrup, Mother Bailey's Quieting Syrup, Daffy's Elixir and Atkinson's Infants' Preservative.

The reasons for these quite extraordinary sale volumes are not hard to discern, since laudanum sold for one penny for an ounce, half the price of a pint of beer. Opium was used for a whole range of ailments from coughs and colds to rheumatism, and a remedy for piles comprised laudanum and egg yolk in an ointment. It was also much used for controlling the symptoms of the very prevalent dysentery and cholera, and to keep babies quiet.

To make ends meet, many wives worked in the mills and other factories of the big industrial centres, and they had to pay for the care of their small children. The baby minders would often reduce the cost of their services if the parents provided them with so called 'quietening mixture', and the constant dosing of the children with opium often led to malnutrition due to an associated disinclination to eat.

In a report to the Privy Council in 1862, a Dr Edward Greenhow suggested that the high rates of infant mortality in these big cities was as much to do with malnutrition as it was to dysentery and infections, though he might have added that opium was also implicated in the accidental or deliberate overdosing of children.

The eating of opium was also common in certain parts of the country, especially the Fens, north from Cambridge to the Wash. This was allegedly because rheumatism was prevalent in this part of Britain and the many agricultural workers used it to ease their pains, but it was probably also to alleviate the misery of their lives in what was then a damp and dreary part of Britain. The overall level of opium dependence can only be guessed at, but was probably quite high.

The popularity of opium in 18th and 19th century Britain supported a huge supply and distribution network, and this had its origins in the highly profitable activities of the East India Company. This venerable body was originally heavily involved in the supply of opium to China and thus responsible, in part, for the abuses of opium in that country.

Opium was almost certainly present in China from as early as the first century AD. Before the 16th century it was mainly used for medicinal purposes, though there was some recreational use. It was usually taken by mouth, as in India and Turkey, the bitter taste masked by the addition of various spices like nutmeg, cardamom and cinnamon.

The smoking of opium was unknown in China until Portuguese, Spanish and Dutch traders took advantage of the earlier discoveries in the Americas and introduced the tobacco habit into their colonies in India, Indonesia and the Philippines, and subsequently into China and Japan, from the late 16th century. The Chinese embraced this new habit with enthusiasm and tobacco smoking became a real social problem, so much so that in the early 17th century it was banned for a while.

It was the vacuum produced by this ban that opened the way for the introduction of opium smoking, initially as a mixture with tobacco. Opium shops and dens quickly appeared in most towns to cater for the growing number of addicts. The smoker inhaled the fumes from a globule of molten opium held in the bowl of a bamboo pipe that was heated in a flame, and these fumes were then held in the lungs for as long as possible before expulsion through the nostrils. Serious smokers would take as many as four pipes in quick succession before succumbing to a deep and troubled sleep (narcosis) for periods lasting from 15 minutes to several hours. They would then awaken without apparent ill effects.

The trade in opium was initially dominated by the Portuguese via their settlements in Goa, after which the Dutch took over using their colonies in Java. Finally the British dominated the trade, using the agents and ships of the British East India Company. This hugely successful trading operation had been established in 1600 through a charter issued by Elizabeth I, and awarded (by the British Government) exclusive trading rights with all lands 'beyond the Cape of Good Hope and the Magellan Straits'. The importance of the opium trade to the EIC was forcefully demonstrated when the Governor General, Warren Hastings, established a state monopoly in November 1773. This required all Indian poppy growers to sell their produce to the company. However, to preserve the Indian labour force from this addictive and debilitating product, all the product had to be exported. Warren Hastings famously stated:

Opium is not a necessity of life but a pernicious article of luxury, which ought not be permitted except for the purposes of foreign commerce only, and which the wisdom of the Government should carefully restrain from internal consumption.

Such two-faced behaviour was unfortunately all too common in dealings between officials of the EIC and its colonial partners and employees.

By the end of the 18th century China was importing more than 2000 chests of opium - perhaps 125 tons – and by the 1760s around 1% of the population were addicted. By 1840 more than 40,000 chests of opium a year were imported, at a cost to the Chinese exchequer of five million silver dollars.

The Chinese authorities, alarmed by this outflow of bullion and by the levels of addiction, made efforts to halt the trade. Emperor Kia King banned importation in 1799, but this had little affect due to organised smuggling involving the various importers and corrupt Chinese officials. However, this did cause aggravation for the EIC and its agents in Canton, since the company could not directly contravene the ban. They got round it by selling their opium to so-called Free Traders in Calcutta, who were mainly English and Scottish entrepreneurs, and the Free Traders organised onward shipment to China.

Some idea of the success of these operations can be appreciated from figures showing that in 1825 more than 10,000 chests were imported via Lintin, an island off Macao and 80 miles down the Pearl River estuary from Canton. Inward bound ships unloaded their cargoes on to floating hulks which were mainly ex-merchant vessels whose masts had been removed. They were essentially fortified opium warehouses. There was also competition from a growing number of British and American owners of fast opium clippers who carried opium from India to China.

Relations between the Chinese authorities and these traders gradually worsened, and major upset was caused when the Emperor Tao-Kuang sent a newly empowered commissioner, Lin Tse-hsu, to Canton in March 1839 with the authority to seize and destroy all the opium stocks. The European traders refused to comply with his edicts until they received instructions from Lord Palmerston's chief representative, Captain Charles Elliot, a former Royal Navy sea captain, to comply. They duly handed over in excess of 20,000 chests of opium, much of it belonging to the British firm of Jardine, Matheson and Co.

There was method in this apparent madness, since the merchants were overstocked with opium and the price had fallen. They had also received a promise from Queen Victoria's government that they would be indemnified for their losses.

Lin Tse-hsu now found himself with a major problem - the destruction of this contraband. He eventually solved it by stirring the opium with a mixture of salt and lime in water in large trenches. Once the opium had been broken down, the detritus was flushed away into the Pearl River.

Despite this setback, the traders were soon back in business importing opium via ports further up the coast. This precipitated a brief naval skirmish off Hong Kong in September 1839 between the British merchant fleet and blockading Chinese junks. Further naval actions followed, and in April 1840 an expeditionary force of 10,000 men plus eighteen warships were rushed from the colony of Ceylon. The First Opium War commenced in earnest.

This was a very uneven conflict, since there was essentially no Chinese navy, while the British merchant and naval fleets were the strongest in the world. The war dragged on for two years, with a series of small but bloody battles resulting in the capture of Shanghai and the ports of Ningbo, Zhapu and Zhenjiang. In August 1842 the naval forces sailed up the Yangtse River to Nanking (now Nanjing).

The Chinese now sued for peace, and that month a treaty was signed on board HMS *Cornwallis*, the Chinese agreeing to cede the barren island of Hong Kong to the British in perpetuity with a payment of 21 million silver dollars as recompense for the opium destroyed. For the Chinese this was not only a financial disaster but a practical one. Opium imports quickly rose to pre-war levels, and continued to grow to match demand.

Any satisfaction felt by the British War Office was tempered by a growing feeling in Victorian society that the opium trade with China was immoral.

Despite these misgivings, trade with China, especially in opium, continued to expand, and by 1850 75% of Indian opium was passing through the colony of Hong Kong. Following the peace treaty of 1842, Hong Kong had developed rapidly, with all the normal essentials for colonial life including fine houses, shops and brothels, as well as a fine bonded warehouse for the main opium exporter, Jardine, Matheson and Co.

The Americans and the French were also now seeking their share of this lucrative trade, and Britain retaliated by seeking 'most-favoured nation status' from the Chinese in 1854, with demands that the Chinese open all their ports for duty-free importation of British goods. The Chinese refused, and following several incidents, including an attempt to poison much of the European population in Hong Kong, joint military action by the British and French was initiated in what became known as the Second Opium War (1857-1860).

This was a much more bloody conflict than the first war and at its height involved nearly 18,000 allied troops and a naval squadron numbering 173 vessels. It culminated in the capture of Beijing in October 1860 after a pitched battle that matched élite (but doomed) Mongolian cavalry against allied cannons. The allies then looted much of the valuable artwork from the Old Summer Palace before destroying the buildings, though they stopped short of destroying the Forbidden City for fear that such a supreme act of vandalism would jeopardize any hope of bringing the Chinese to the peace table.

In the event, the Chinese were forced to allow further trading opportunities and to officially legalise the opium trade. This lasted right through until 1906, when a decree was issued demanding the immediate closure of all opium dens and the cessation of smoking. Yet even as late as 1930, there were more than 6000 licensed opium dens in South East Asia, 3000 of these in French Indochina.

In the meantime, Chinese migrants had taken their habit with them to the rest of South East Asia, Australia, and across the Pacific to the USA and South America. Tens of thousands of Chinese migrants entered the USA via San Francisco and worked in the Chinese laundries, on the railroads and in the goldfields of California.

Migration into Europe was less common, though opium dens did exist in most of the large cities. As in the USA, they were considered to be centres of vice and prostitution, though seduction was usually the last thing on the minds of the most dedicated opium smokers. It was the artists, poets and writers of the so-called Romantic era (around 1775 to 1835) who adopted opium as their drug of choice. Perhaps most famous of these was Thomas Penson de Quincey (born in Manchester in 1785), whose book *Confessions of an English Opium-Eater* was published in 1822. He seems to have first used the drug in 1804 as a treatment for toothache and facial neuralgia, but the pain relief was but a prelude to a new pleasure. In his book he noted:

That my pains had vanished was now a trifle in my eyes - this negative effect was swallowed up in the immensity of those positive effects which had opened before me - in the abyss of divine enjoyment thus suddenly revealed. Here was a panacea... for all human woes; here was the secret of happiness.

De Quincey began taking laudanum on a regular basis to counteract the pain of a gastric ulcer, but found that it also enhanced his enjoyment of weekly trips to the opera. In publicising how the drug enhanced his 'sensual pleasure' in music, he undoubtedly encouraged others to experiment with the drug, just as later generations would use LSD or marijuana for enhancement of sensual experiences. The section of his book entitled '*The Pleasures of Opium*' contained very strong endorsements for the advantages of opium use compared with alcohol consumption:

Wine disorders the mental faculties, opium on the contrary introduces among them the most exquisite order, legislation, and harmony. Wine robs a man of his self-possession: opium greatly invigorates it.

However, de Quincey's experimentation was soon out of hand. By 1815 he was taking 8000 drops of laudanum each day and had descended into penury, with nightmarish visions of being 'buried, for 1000 years, in stone coffins, with mummies and sphinxes... I was kissed, with cancerous kisses, by crocodiles; and laid, confounded with all unutterable slimy things amongst reeds and Nilotic mud'. It was to revive his fortunes that he wrote the Confessions. The book was popular not least because it captured the imagination of a literature-loving middle class who revelled in tales of roguish behaviour and rebellion.

Despite his reputation as a reprobate, de Quincey appears to have been a sensitive and generous man, who became very friendly with both William and Dorothy Wordsworth and the Coleridges. At one point he lent money to Coleridge, and he became particularly fond of the Wordsworth children. His familiarity with their lives and literary works allowed him to write critical accounts of these important poets which helped enhance their reputations.

There were several editions of his book, which eventually grew to twice its original length. De Quincey was reviled and admired in equal measure for his admissions, but the proceeds from the book certainly allowed him to lead a reasonably happy life, and eventually he managed to reduce his consumption of opium from 320 grains a day (about 8000 drops) to 12 grains (around 300 drops). He clearly suffered severe withdrawal effects during this process and wrote of *the torments of a man passing out of one mode of existence into another*. He died in 1859 at the age of 74 years, which was a good age considering his abuses. His near-contemporary, the poet Samuel Taylor Coleridge, was not so lucky.

Like de Quincey, Coleridge began taking laudanum not just as a treatment for neuralgia and toothache but to alleviate the symptoms of dysentery. His consumption of the drug increased dramatically in 1802 as he began to treat himself for a back condition, and he became increasingly miserable from what he described as 'the worst and most degrading of slaveries'. He was certainly not helped by the time he spent with Thomas Beddoes of Bristol, who experimented in his 'Pneumatic Institute' with opium, henbane, cannabis, and even nitrous oxide.

On innumerable occasions Coleridge tried to break himself of the habit. He was, from 1816 to 1828, a tenant of the physician James Gillman in Highgate, London, who tried to wean him off laudanum, little realising that his patient was being supplied secretly by a local druggist. At times he was consuming as much as two pints (perhaps 20,000 drops) of laudanum each week. And yet he managed to produce some stunning poetry, including his best known works *The Rime of the Ancient Mariner* and *Kubla Khan*. Although the latter was often considered a classic example of a work inspired by opium, this has now been discounted.

Coleridge's plight was perhaps best summarised by the author Sir Walter Scott when he claimed that Coleridge was 'a man of genius struggling with bad habits'. When he died in 1834 (aged 62) he left a written plea that others might learn from his mistakes:

After my death, I earnestly entreat that a full and unqualified narrative of my wretchedness, and of its guilty cause, may be made public, that at least some little good may be affected by the direful example.

The poets Byron, Shelley, Keats and Southey were all moderate consumers of opium, though only Keats makes much mention of it in *Ode to a Nightingale*:

My heart aches, and a drowsy numbness pains
My sense, as though of hemlock I had drunk,
Or emptied some dull opiate to the drains.

And in *The Eve of St. Agnes*:

In sort of wakeful swoon, perplex'd she lay,
Until the poppied warmth of sleep oppress'd
Her sooth'd limbs, and soul fatigued away.

Elizabeth Barrett, later to become the wife of the poet Robert Browning, appears to have become a regular user of opium at the age of fifteen as the result of a painful spinal condition. For her it was an 'elixir because the tranquilising power has been so great'. Later she claimed 'I think better of sleep than I ever did, now that she will not come near me except in a red hood of poppies'.

Her condition was never completely diagnosed and the pain was often so great that she complained 'opium, opium - night after night – and some nights even opium won't do'. She none the less produced some very well-regarded poetry, some of which bears the hallmarks of opium intoxication.

Across the English Channel, opium use was no less common. The French poet Charles Baudelaire was first induced to take the drug as a treatment for the syphilis he acquired as a young man. He is reputed to have told his mother 'When I was very young I got poxed'. In his poem *La Chambre Double* he compares the lures and perils of women and opium:

> *Here in this world, cramped but so disgusting,*
> *Only one familiar object cheers me:*
> *The phial of laudanum;*
> *An old and terrifying friend;*
> *Like all women, alas,*
> *Prolific in caresses and betrayals.*

As for writers of prose, Wilkie Collins was possibly the most conspicuous of the opium addicts. His most famous novel, The *Moonstone*, was probably composed almost wholly under the influence of the drug and it was his secretary who wrote the actual words in 1868 as he dictated to her. Certainly the plot relies very heavily on the theft of a large Hindu diamond carried out while the thief is under the influence of opium. Collins made no secret of his addiction and carried a hip flask of laudanum wherever he went describing himself as someone for whom 'laudanum – divine laudanum' was his only friend. He was also one of the first of the writers to take injections of morphine, ostensibly to break him of the habit of drinking laudanum. In a letter to a friend he reported:

My doctor is trying to break me of the habit of drinking laudanum. I am stabbed every night at ten with a sharp-pointed syringe which injects morphia under my skin – and gets me a good night's rest without any of the drawbacks of taking opium internally.

Despite this opiate abuse, which probably commenced as a treatment for his rheumatism and gout in 1862, he none the less survived until 1889 and died aged 65 years.

One 19th century writer and poet who is invariably mentioned whenever drugs and literature are linked is Aleister Crowley (born 1875 in Leamington Spa). He is probably most remembered for his interests in the occult and mysticism which he claimed were initiated following a 'visitation' by the goddess Nuit while he was on holiday in Egypt in 1904. He was also the author of books with titles like *Magick without Tears* and *Diary of a Drug Fiend*, and some poetry, of which *White Stains*, published in 1898, is probably the most infamous. It was a collection of pornographic verse and was immediately banned.

Crowley fuelled a libidinous and bisexual lifestyle with alcohol, opium, heroin, cocaine, hashish, mescaline and even ether, and had the dubious honour of being immortalised in Somerset Maughan's 1908 novel *The Magician* and appearing among that famous collection of persons on the Beatles' *Sergeant Pepper* LP sleeve. Despite his dissolute lifestyle, he survived to the ripe old age of 72.

Other 19th century novelists probably took opium occasionally for pain and described their experiences of seeing the darker side of life in the ghettos of, for example, London in the cases of Charles Dickens (*the Mystery of Edwin Drood*) and Oscar Wilde (*the Picture of Dorian Gray*):

Dorian winced, and looked round at the grotesque things that lay in such
fantastic postures on the ragged mattresses. The twisted limbs, the gaping
mouths, the staring lustreless eyes fascinated him. He knew in what strange
heavens they were suffering, and what dull hells were teaching them the
secret of some new joy.

The Royal Family was also familiar with opium and other
substances, as the records of the local pharmacy near Balmoral have
recently revealed. For George IV substance abuse became a way of
life, and his binge drinking of opium and cherry brandy mixtures,
together with his gluttony, hastened his descent into invalid status,
though he somehow managed to survive to 68.

One further supposed attribute of opium was its ability to control
what the leading physician Sir Almroth Wright described in 1912 as
a woman's 'periodically recurring phases of hypersensitiveness,
unreasonableness, and loss of the sense of proportion'. These
problems were because 'the physiology and psychology of women is
full of difficulties'. He expounded these views initially in a letter to
The Times in March 1912 and then in expanded form in a treatise
entitled '*The Unexpurgated Case Against Woman Suffrage*', published
in 1913.

Similarly misogynistic views and assertions appeared in the
medical textbooks of the time; those of the gynaecologist Dr Henry
McNaughton Jones are particularly extreme. His textbook *Diseases*
of Women went through nine editions, and revealed the particular
challenges of the unmarried woman who he believed to be generally
neurotic and who harboured 'erotic thoughts, desires and practices
that still further enervate her nervous systems and enfeeble her
central control'. Married women were no less problematic with their
'congestive dysmenorrhoea and overalgia, her uterus may be as flabby
as her brain, and her ovary be as fertile in aches as her imagination is

in fanciful illusions'. These conditions might be treated with opium though, were, he believed more often caused by dependence on it.

Certainly there was a large number of middle-class Victorian wives for whom opium provided a release from boredom and frustration. For many Victorians, both male and female, opium use was as common as their use of tobacco.

These literary experiences and other excesses were made possible by the almost unlimited access to poisons and potions during Victorian times. Opium use was not regulated in Britain before the Poisons and Pharmacy Act of 1868, and supplies of the drug poured in from Turkey and India. There are records from 1830 showing that around 190,000lb of opium was imported into England (97% from Turkey), while by 1900 the amount had risen to around 620,000lb (74% from Turkey, 12% from India and lesser amounts from Persia and France). Major wholesalers included William Allen and Company of Plough Lane, London (later to become part of Allen and Hanburys and then Glaxo), and Thomas Morson and Sons of Fleet Market, London. These supplied the provincial apothecaries and thence the corner shops whose owners had little knowledge of the drug they were selling – often to children who had been sent on an errand to buy a 'penny stick of opium'.

With the establishment of the Pharmaceutical Society of Great Britain in 1841 (allegedly by a group of London chemists and druggists who met in the Crown and Anchor tavern in the Strand), a new view of opium use began to emerge that questioned its safety. There were special concerns with regard to accidental overdose, suicide (though throat cutting and hanging were the favoured methods), murder and the ever-present problem of adulteration – Turkish opium regularly contained quantities of cow dung, poppy capsule material and even gravel. Attempts were made to weed out charlatans and the Pharmaceutical Society Bill of 1851 stated that:

It should not be lawful for any person to carry on the business of a chemist and druggist... unless such a person shall be a pharmaceutical chemist.

The Poisons and Pharmacy Act of 1868 led to the introduction of formal registration for pharmacists, after special examinations. In addition, opium was officially identified as a potential poison which required appropriate labelling, though patent medicines were excluded from the bill and this loophole allowed the famous Dr Collis Browne's chlorodyne to remain on sale. This mixture of chloroform, opium and (usually) cannabis, launched in 1856, was in use for everything from cholera to flatulence, with some people consuming several pints each week. Certainly the dangers of addiction were well understood, and these were clearly enunciated in Louis Lewin's *Phantastica: Narcotic and Stimulating drugs.*

The drug (opium) must be injected more frequently and in larger quantities, the chain of slavery becomes shorter and tugs at the morphinist... the brain cells grow restive, demand satisfaction, shriek, and revenge themselves by producing pain if they are not satisfied quickly enough.

Against this background of widespread use and abuse, most of the groundbreaking scientific studies on the chemical constituents of opium took place during the 19th century. The French pharmacist Armand Séguin was probably the first to isolate morphine in crystalline form, in 1804. He described his work to the Institut de France in Paris under the title *Sur l'Opium*, but he made no written report before 1814. So it was the German Friedrich Wilhelm Sertürner, a young pharmacist's assistant with no formal scientific training, who is usually given the credit for the first isolation of morphine.

Sertürner reported his discovery, which he called 'morphium' after the Greek god of sleep Morpheus, in a relatively obscure journal –

the Journal der Pharmacie – in 1806. He and three associates went on to experiment with this new crystalline substance, and he evidently experienced many of the side-effects of the large doses he is reputed to have taken. He reported these new results in the journal *Annalen der Physik* in 1817, concluding with the warning: 'I consider it my duty to attract attention to the terrible effects of this new substance in order that calamity may be averted'. Clearly this advice did not reach the great majority of 19th century society, but the article was spotted by the great French chemist Joseph Louis Gay Lussac, who had it reprinted in French in one of the major chemical journals - the *Annales de Chimie* – and also took the liberty of renaming the substance 'morphine'.

However, the commercial production of pure morphine was not possible until William Gregory of the University of Edinburgh perfected a method of extraction and purification in 1831. It was then produced in bulk by Macfarlan and Co. of Edinburgh.

While writers and others continued their love affair with laudanum, the medical profession turned increasingly to pure morphine. Administration of the drug was facilitated by the invention of the hypodermic syringe and needle by Alexander Wood of Edinburgh in 1853, and later modifications made by Charles Hunter of St George's Hospital London ensured that casualties of the two great wars of the mid-19th century – the American Civil War and the Crimean War – could receive pain relief in an efficient manner.

Huge quantities of opium were also dispensed to treat dysentery, and many of the soldiers returned home with an opium habit. For many of these returning soldiers, consumption of opium was also a way of forgetting the horrors and savagery of the conflicts in which they had fought.

Both the British and American governments began to seek ways of curbing the illicit trade in opium. After several failed attempts, the new Liberal Government of 1893 tabled a motion that:

The Indo-Chinese opium trade is morally indefensible, and requests Her Majesty's Government to take such steps as might be necessary for bringing about its speedy close.

In the same year, Gladstone's government set up a Royal Commission to establish the facts about opium use and abuse, especially with regard to the production of Indian opium. The Commission heard evidence from 723 people and reported its findings in 1895. Overall it concluded that it was unnecessary to prohibit the production of Indian opium, not least because there would be a huge loss of revenue for the British Government. It would also represent an unacceptable act of prohibition for the Indian people. The many Indian consumers of opium were reported to be 'hale and hearty, fit for work and whose habit did not interfere with their longevity or health'. The report further declared that 'there was no such thing as a murderous opium maniac'.

The British settlements in Asia had for years been heavily dependent upon the opium trade, and despite legislation from the House of Commons in 1908 which effectively closed the opium dens in Hong Kong and Ceylon, opium use was not declared illegal until 1945 – 103 years after Hong Kong had been ceded to the British following the end of the first Opium War in 1842. Making a drug illegal does not guarantee its elimination, and in the mid-1970s there were an estimated 30,000 opium smokers and 120,000 heroin users in Hong Kong, requiring in excess of 35 tons of opium to satisfy their habit.

Similar grand plans for the complete eradication of opium use in China were initiated following an imperial decree in 1906 banning opium smoking and seeking the closure of all opium dens by 1917. However, these remained as merely fine intentions as long as cultivation of opium continued apace in India and what became known as the Golden Triangle – a temperate region 1000m above sea level and of 225,000 square kilometres between the borders of Thailand, Burma and Laos.

In fact near anarchy in the opium trade existed throughout the first half of the twentieth century. This was especially true in China, where local warlords controlled the trade, and following the invasion of Manchuria by the Japanese in 1931, production was further encouraged. Throughout this Japanese incursion and right through to the arrival of the communist government of Mao Tse-tung in 1950, the nationalist government of Chiang Kai-shek relied upon opium revenues for its very survival. Not surprisingly, by the end of the 1930s, possibly as many as 10% of the Chinese population were opium addicts.

Elsewhere in South East Asia, the French colonial forces had also been involved in the opium trade for many decades, initially in Cambodia and Laos, then later in Vietnam. An undoubted early champion of this opium trade was the first Governor-General of French Indochina, Paul Doumer, who after his appointment in 1897 set about the total reorganisation of opium production, starting with the construction of a new opium refinery in Saigon. The revenues from this trade very rapidly generated enough money to pay for much of the development of their colonial territories. Interestingly, Paul Doumer entered politics on his return to France in 1902, rising to become President of France in May 1931, only to be assassinated by an unhinged Russian émigré one year later.

By the end of WWII, production in Laos, with French co-operation, probably exceeded 30 tons per year. Following the removal of official French Government support in 1946, French military intelligence took over support of the opium trade. These intelligence operatives developed a hugely successful liaison with the Hmong hill tribes of Laos, who not only provided the raw opium (their only cash crop), but with French munitions acted as an effective guerrilla force (maquis) to combat the emerging liberation army of Vietnam. This trade took on an international complexion, with the help of Corsican gangsters working out of Laos and Vietnam and collaborating with their compatriots, based initially in Corsica but later in the city of Marseille.

This opium was soon finding its way to the streets of New York and other European capitals. However, 80 years of French colonial involvement in Indochina came to an abrupt end in May 1954 when a powerful Viet-Minh army of 50,000 surrounded and defeated a French army of more than 15,000 at Dien Bien Phu on the border between Laos and North Vietnam. The armistice signed in Geneva allowed the French to retain hold of South Vietnam (south of the 17th parallel) while an election was called to decide who would control a reunified Vietnam. However, a bloody civil war erupted in Saigon in early 1955, and the French Government finally lost its enthusiasm for their Indochina colonies and withdrew in April 1956. They left behind several hundred (mainly) Corsican gangsters, who ran what became known as Air Opium, a collective name for a number of small airlines servicing the opium trade and making regular flights between Laos and South Vietnam.

Various international meetings were convened between the world wars to try to curb the spread of narcotics, but these were mostly inconclusive or had no real power. During this inter-war period opium production increased dramatically in Persia, much of the Balkans and in Turkey. Finally, the UN Fund for Drug Control was set up in 1971. Unfortunately it has been as ineffective in controlling drugs as its parent body has been in its efforts to stop wars and prevent famine. In fairness these worthy bodies were not operating on a level playing field, because many governments, especially in South East Asia, relied on the revenues from the opium trade, and received assistance from various clandestine organisations which allegedly included French military intelligence and the CIA.

The arrival of the communists in China heralded the dawn of CIA involvement in South East Asia, because although the Americans had supported the Nationalist Army of Chiang Kia-shek (the Kuomintang or KMT) in their fight against the Japanese, there was now a need to halt the anticipated spread of communism in this part of the world. They supported the residual units of the KMT on the border between Burma and China, and the CIA airline – initially Civil Air Transport (1950) but later (1959) renamed Air America – not only supplied the KMT with arms and ammunition but allegedly helped with the transportation of opium.

Initially the KMT made brave but futile efforts to invade China, but it quickly realised that this was a fruitless enterprise and settled for the highly lucrative opium trade. In the 1950s this amounted to around 80 tons per annum, but by the early 1960s total production amounted to 300-400 tons per annum. The KMT were not the only producers of opium, since both the Thai and Burmese governments supported a lucrative trade in the drug. Possibly with CIA support, the military rulers in Thailand had by 1955 turned Bangkok into one of the world's chief trading centres for opium. The total opium production of the Golden Triangle at the end of the 1960s was probably 1200-1400 tons.

CHAPTER FOUR

A DEADLY INDUSTRY

Heroin

The scene was set for the emergence of a new and much more dangerous trade based upon the morphine derivative heroin. This drug is an even more effective means of pain relief – and abuse – than its parent opium or morphine.

Diacetyl morphine (later to be called heroin) was first prepared by the pharmacist Alder Wright working at St Mary's Hospital Paddington in 1874. Seeking a non-addictive alternative to morphine, he simply boiled morphine with acetic anhydride to produce a new crystalline product. This was administered to dogs and shown to induce drowsiness and vomiting, and although a number of reports of this new narcotic appeared in journals, little attention was paid to the discovery.

It was resurrected in 1898 by the German chemist Heinrich Dreser, chief pharmacologist of the Bayer company at Elberfeld, who was greatly impressed by its analgesic properties. It was Dreser who christened the new drug; the name is based on the German word *heroisch*.

In addition to its use as an extremely potent painkiller, what elevates heroin to the status of a major drug of abuse is its ease of preparation using simple and cheap chemicals. Raw opium is dissolved in hot water and then treated with lime to precipitate the calcium salts of organic acids that are present as impurities, and these are filtered off. The residual solution is then carefully acidified and the crude morphine precipitates; this is what is termed 'morphine base' and represents about 10% of the weight of the raw opium.

Now the conversion into heroin can commence. The morphine is simply heated with acetic anhydride, usually in a glass vessel, for a number of hours at 85 degrees Centigrade to effect the conversion. Water is added, then the mixture is neutralised with washing soda (sodium carbonate) and the heroin precipitates. This is typically sold as 'brown sugar' and contains about 30-40% of heroin (number 3 grade), so it is only suitable for smoking. It can be further purified by recrystallisation using alcohol and ether mixtures and activated charcoal, or converted into its water soluble hydrochloride salt. The heroin is now of 80-100% purity and is suitable for injecting (number 4 grade).

These procedures are so simple and the chemicals so readily available that it is all too easy to see how it became part of the cottage industries in Burma, Afghanistan and, in particular, the backstreets of Marseille and Hong Kong.

The involvement of heroin gangs in Marseille is familiar to most people, thanks to the success of the films French Connection and French Connection II, but the origins of this trade are even more fascinating than these semi-factual stories. The era of prohibition in the US had encouraged the formation of criminal gangs which dealt in alcohol and narcotics, though interestingly the Mafia were originally only involved in the first of these activities, since at this time certain family values were still respected and the Mafia 'families' would not become involved in narcotics or prostitution. However, they observed the vast sums of money being made by less scrupulous syndicates and soon became involved in this growing business opportunity. From the early 1930s, a new breed of Mafiosi led by ruthless gangsters like Charles 'Lucky' Luciano emerged in New York City to dominate the closely-connected trades in narcotics and prostitution, and this continued essentially unchecked until WWII, even though Luciano was imprisoned in 1936.

The Mafia had not had such an easy time in Italy, because Mussolini had initiated a crackdown in the late 1920s, and by the start of WWII there was only limited narcotics activity in Sicily. However, Mafia fortunes revived following the liberation of Sicily from the Germans in 1943, when the US Government's Office of Strategic Studies (OSS) – the forerunner of the Central Intelligence Agency – helped to install some of the local Mafia bosses in key political positions in order to frustrate the growing influence of the local communists.

In 1946, Lucky Luciano was freed from jail and deported to Sicily. He and other senior Mafiosi were then in a position to facilitate the growth of heroin factories on the island to supply the growing demands for the drug from the USA and Canada. By 1948 most of the heroin smuggled into North America was derived from crude Turkish opium that had been shipped via the Lebanon to Sicily or into Marseille for chemical transformation into heroin. The Corsican narcotics gangs in Marseille had a long history in purifying crude Turkish opium, and during the period 1950 to 1970, the Mafia and Corsican syndicates agreed to share the American market with an increasing number of laboratories established in Marseille and controlled by the powerful Corsican families.

What is remarkable is that although the French police managed to close more than a dozen of these factories, others remained in operation throughout the 1960s. While some inertia was doubtless due to police corruption in Marseille, the supposition has always been that the French Government tolerated this highly damaging industry because the Corsican syndicates were useful paid participants in violent struggles against the strong local communist unions. These unions were so strong in 1950 that they were able to close the port of Marseille completely, which effectively prevented military supplies leaving for Indochina, where the French Army was involved in its increasingly desperate struggle with the Viet-Minh. The strike was eventually broken after violent clashes with the Corsican gangsters.

At the height of their activities in Marseille during the mid 1960s, it has been estimated that there were around 20-25 laboratories in the city each producing 50-150 kg of heroin per month, most of it destined for the major cities of the USA and Canada. However, two factors conspired to end this domination of the heroin market in the early 1970s. Firstly the Turkish Government was persuaded by the Nixon Administration to introduce a successful ban on opium production, and secondly the French Government – again under pressure from the US - began to apply much greater pressure on the gangs. These were quite rapidly forced out of the city and transferred their activities to Indochina. The message from Richard Nixon to the American people and to his allies abroad concerning his war on drugs and other aberrant behaviour was simple:

Do you think the Russians allow dope? Hell no... homosexuality, dope, immorality in general – these are the enemies of strong societies.

It is interesting to compare the activities of the heroin gangs in Marseille with their counterparts in Hong Kong. This island outpost of the British Empire had a long history of opium production, and from the 1960s became a major centre of heroin production rivalling Marseille. At this time, much of the opium from the Golden Triangle passed through Thai ports and thence by trawler to Hong Kong for processing. Most of the criminal gangs had learned their trade in Shanghai between the wars, and were only displaced from Shanghai when it became clear that the communist forces of Mao Tse-tung were going to occupy the city in the late 1940s. Between the wars, the so-called Green Gang (*qingbang*) monopolised the opium trade in Shanghai with as many as 100,000 gang members by 1920, and up to 40,000 chests of Persian, Turkish, Indian, and Chinese opium passing through Hong Kong each year. Most of the heroin users smoked heroin rather than injecting it, since they had easy access to grade 3 drug (around 40% heroin). Lumps of the drug were typically placed on to aluminium foil and heated with a flame, then the smoke was inhaled via a rolled-up sheet of paper. This was known as 'chasing the dragon'.

After the end of the Second World War, the Americans were especially sensitive to the need for influence in South East Asia as they feared the expansion of communism. In response to this perceived threat, the Truman administration transformed the wartime OSS into the CIA, with a two-fold mission in espionage and covert operations. Interestingly, the OSS had supported the newly formed Viet-Minh and its leaders Ho Chi Minh and General Vo Nguyen Giap when they had fought the Japanese during the closing months of WWII. This support was withdrawn once it became clear that the French were going to try to regain their colonial empire by waging an anti-communist crusade against the forces of Ho Chi Minh and General Giap. However, these French aspirations were ended at the battle of Dien Bien Phu in 1954.

The CIA operated first in Burma during the 1950s, then Laos in the 1960s, and after the French colonial forces finally left Indochina in mid 1956, the CIA had the field to themselves. From 1959 to 1970, the CIA used the planes of Air America to help maintain a guerrilla army comprising as many as 45,000 of the local Hmong tribespeople.

The origins of Air America are very interesting. The airline started life as the private airforce of the American General Claire Chennault, whose Flying Tigers supported Chiang Kai-shek and his forces (KMT) in their struggles with the Japanese during WWII. At the end of the war Chennault continued to support the KMT and other forces opposed to the communist regime, and the CIA then purchased his Civil Air Transport, renaming it Air America. The Hmong tribespeople were now tasked with putting pressure on the communist Pathet Lao forces who operated near the border of Laos and North Vietnam, and were increasingly supported by the armed forces of North Vietnam. Arms, food and medical supplies were shipped to the villages of the Hmong fighters, and opium reputedly made its way back to the cities of Long Tieng and Vientiane and thence to Saigon and onwards to the international market.

The role of Air America and the agents of the CIA in opium smuggling have been a hotly-debated issue over many years. Most of the books written about the history of the CIA imply with varying levels of veracity that opium was frequently carried out of Laos on Air America planes, though CIA chiefs over the years have always denied that the pilots and CIA operatives were aware of these cargoes*. The gung ho activities of Mel Gibson and his fellow actors in the 1990 film *Air America* are certainly not credible and caused the CIA a serious degree of distress.

The success of the opium trade was dealt a bitter blow when the Americans decided to bomb the Pathet Lao into submission in 1964, and the resultant instability amongst the native opium growers led to a major fall in production. Even so in 1969 it is likely that the region of the Golden Triangle still produced around 1000 tons of raw opium, and the heroin trade was about to receive a major boost as the Americans moved into Vietnam with a vengeance.

(*In Anthony McCoy's 700 page book The Politics of Heroin, he gives a comprehensive account of his views on CIA complicity in the global drug trade especially in Afghanistan, South East Asia and South America. He spent part of 1971 with the Hmong tribespeople, so his account has to be given serious consideration. Interestingly, the most recent book (also 700 pages long) about the CIA – Legacy of Ashes by the journalist Tim Weiner (2007) – makes no mention at all of Air America, and the index to the book has no entries for opium, heroin or cocaine. Despite extensive coverage of CIA activities in Afghanistan, there is no mention of the number one crop of that country, Papaver somniferum. The contrast between these two books could not be more stark.)

American experts had already been playing a leading role as advisors to the South Vietnamese army, filling the vacuum left by the withdrawal of the French colonial forces in 1956, with the aim of ensuring the survival of the anti-communist government of Ngo Dinh Diem. But the US Government found itself dragged ever more deeply into the quagmire that became the Vietnam War, with significant numbers of troops involved from 1963 to 1973. At its height half a million US military personnel were engaged in fighting the North Vietnamese army and their allies the Viet-Minh (called the Viet Cong by the US and the government of Diem). A very large number of US combatants ended up smoking dope of various kinds, primarily heroin and marijuana, and the quality of the heroin was amazing in both its purity and its relative cheapness.

The criminal gangs in Hong Kong were not slow to exploit the arrival of tens of thousands of potential customers, and at least 21 specialised chemistry laboratories (staffed with Hong Kong expert chemists) were installed in the Golden Triangle to service the GI market. These reputedly produced as much as 1200 tons of heroin per year. At least 15 of these supplied the highest grade heroin, which the service personnel usually smoked in admixture with tobacco and marijuanha.

At the height of the conflict around 15-20% of combatants were addicted in some measure to heroin, and an official report estimated that one in three had used it. If they survived their tour of duty, many of the GIs took the habit home with them. It is intriguing to note that the American military has always maintained stringent controls over the drinking of alcohol by servicemen under age 21, yet most of the conscripts were only 19, and the sheer volume and accessibility of drugs in Vietnam inevitably led these young men to use them in place of alcohol. They were assailed on all sides by street vendors and civilian workers in their barracks, all ready to supply small quantities of heroin.

The widespread use of drugs, and an overwhelming sense that they were losing the war, led to a collapse of morale by the early 1970s, leading the then US commander General Creighton Abrahams to note in 1971:

I've got white shirts all over the place – psychologists, drugs counsellors, detox specialists, rehab. people... is this a goddamned army or a mental hospital!

The US forces seem to have been particularly handicapped by the activities of the Vietnamese Air Force and Navy, which probably devoted as much time to drug smuggling as they did to fighting the enemy. Indeed it has been claimed that the South Vietnamese airforce C-47 transport planes flew into Saigon's main airbase loaded with Laotian opium throughout the war years.

The eventual departure of the American forces from Vietnam after January 1973 left something of a vacuum for the narcotics gangs, but they quickly adapted to this change of fortune and turned their attentions to Europe and the Americas, using initially Bangkok and then Hong Kong as their gateways for exporting heroin. However, the new communist governments of South East Asia were not always so tolerant of opium production and refinement, and an increasing amount of opium production transferred to Mexico, Afghanistan, Pakistan and even Iran. The revolution in January 1979 that led to the overthrow of the Shah of Iran produced an unexpected boost to opium production, since the Ayatollah Khomeini and his followers were much more opposed to alcohol than they were to narcotics, and the Shah's ban on opium production was reversed.

It was however Afghanistan where most of the opium was produced. Afghanistan had been a major producer of opium for hundreds of years, but now took centre stage in both geopolitics and the drugs trade. This country of 250,000 square kilometres (about the size of Texas) has been fought over for more than 2500 years, and for its many tribes and ethnic groups, opium growing and the repulsion of invaders have always been a way of life. The old Soviet Union had long recognised that this unstable neighbour was a breeding ground for Muslim extremists who could easily upset the delicate balance of its own multi-ethnic state. So from 1965 the Soviet government actively supported the emerging neo-communist People's Democratic Party of Afghanistan (PDPA), and this body finally seized power following a coup in April 1978.

The PDPA's proposed reforms included equal rights, education for women and major land reforms that would have overturned centuries of male-dominated socioeconomic structure. Not surprisingly a revolution began almost at once, and there were mass desertions from the Afghan Army. The Soviet leadership was now under pressure on two fronts – its favoured government was in serious trouble and they were also apprehensive about US plans for Afghanistan now that Iran had become militantly anti-American. Invasion became inevitable and the Russian army rolled into Kabul on Christmas Eve 1979, little realising that this would precipitate a holy war (*jihad*) and the mobilisation of all of the Afghan tribes and ethnic groups. From every mosque and meeting place, thousands of mullahs promulgated the eviction of the invader by whatever means. For the freedom fighters or *mujahideen* this was merely the latest and most powerful invader in their long history of conflict. As in all such conflicts powerful and charismatic leaders emerged, and the two most prominent were Ahmad Massoud, leader of what became known as the Northern Alliance, and Osama bin Laden, who led a group based in Pakistan from about 1982.

The Soviet invasion of Afghanistan was viewed by the US Government as a Soviet threat to the Persian Gulf oil fields, so the CIA and other military units were soon involved. At the height of the war as many as 30,000 mujahideen, armed with American weapons, were in combat. The CIA played the same kind of role as they had in Burma, supporting the local mujahideen guerrillas with armaments as they divided their time between the opium trade and fighting the forces of the Soviet Union. As part of the hundreds of millions of dollars worth of munitions the US supplied, more than 2000 Stinger anti-aircraft missiles were given to the mujahideen. These shoulder-held, heat-seeking missiles turned the tide in the conflict, and morale in the Soviet army and air force collapsed as more than 270 aircraft were brought down in 1987 alone.

Altogether at least 14,000 Russians lost their lives during the conflict, and the real figure may be twice that number. By May 1988, the Soviet government had lost heart and a slow withdrawal began, which was complete by February 1989. This left behind a power vacuum which led inevitably to a vicious and protracted civil war. Initially, Massoud's Northern Alliance was the dominant force, but it gradually gave way to bin Laden's new Taliban, which emerged from the southern part of Afghanistan and was strongly supported by Pakistan. The Taliban finally took Kabul in September 1996, and the Northern Alliance retreated to their strongholds and poppy fields in the north of the country.

Once in command, the Taliban proceeded to impose a tax of 5-10% on all opium harvested and a separate tax on heroin production and shipment. At the same time they deplored the consumption of drugs by the Afghan population and encouraged opium and heroin exports. As Afghanistan became one of the world's leading suppliers, the annual income for the Taliban has been estimated to have reached $8 billion.

Periodically the Taliban leadership made overtures to the United Nations, promising to eradicate opium production in return for recognition of the régime and humanitarian aid. Initially these overtures went unanswered, but following a disastrous opium harvest in 2000 Mullah Omar increased his bid for recognition by putting into force a total ban on opium production. This was rewarded with $43 million of humanitarian aid. The subsequent ban had the effect of driving opium production into the lands of the Northern Alliance, which was still waging war against the Taliban and had always financed its military activities through sales of opium and heroin.

Interestingly, a further source of income for both the Taliban and Northern Alliance was a 'buy-back' policy for Stinger missiles introduced by the CIA following the departure of the Soviet forces. A price of $80,000 to $150,000 was offered for each recovered missile, and this policy seems to have been partially successful, though in 1996 the CIA admitted that 600 missiles were still missing. This has had the effect of making subsequent military operations in Afghanistan fraught with danger, since most of the missing missiles are undoubtedly in the hands of the Taliban.

Following the events of September 11th 2001 and the invasion and overthrow of the Taliban forces, the Northern Alliance has been able to concentrate on opium production and there has been a resurgence in the opium trade. In 2005 it was estimated that 820 metric tons of illicit opium was produced in Afghanistan, which is more than twice the global need for medical opiates (perhaps 380 metric tons), and Afghanistan now probably supplies around 90% of the world's heroin. Attempts by NATO forces to eradicate the opium crop have usually been counter-productive since the local farmers see this as an evil act by yet another invader. Thus far programmes to encourage the farmers to grow alternative cash crops, like *Artemisia annua*, the source of the anti-malarial drug artemisinin, have been unsuccessful.

All this trafficking in opium, morphine and heroin requires smuggling routes and methods of concealment, and over the years some highly imaginative schemes have been devised. Almost every imaginable hollow object has been used at one time or another, including dolls, boot heels, spare tyres, bicycle frames, plaster casts and screw-in cattle horns. The use of human 'mules' who have swallowed condoms and other sealed receptacles full of drugs is well documented, not least because of the numerous reported deaths following leakage of these containers. Insertion of such packages into the anus or vagina is also well known, though the diplomatic bag has also been used as a safer means of smuggling.

The most frequently-cited example of this practice involved the new Laotian ambassador to France, Prince Sopsaisanna, who arrived in Paris in April 1971 to take up his post. One suitcase from his vast array of luggage was temporarily lost at Orly Airport, and when it reappeared it was opened by customs officers to reveal 60 kg of number 4 heroin. Although this diplomatic *faux pas* was hushed up, the French refused to accept the Prince as an ambassador, and he was ultimately recalled to Laos. However, despite these individual efforts, the majority of large-scale smuggling is carried out by plane, ship or long-distance lorry (eg from Northern Afghanistan into Tajikistan, Uzbekistan, Kazakhstan and onwards through Russia and into Europe), and most countries would admit that they believe up to 90% of drugs that are shipped actually arrive safely. As for the huge sums of money generated through the sale of heroin, these are usually laundered via casinos, *bureaus de change* and other larger-scale illicit banking operations.

So the popularity of the opiates, especially heroin, is undiminished, but all of this begs the question: why are humans affected by morphine and heroin? This question remained unanswered until 1975 when John Hughes and his colleagues at the University of Aberdeen isolated two molecules from pig brain that had opiate-like activity. In fact they were up to 20 times more potent than morphine in several assays and appeared to act at the same biological sites as morphine and related opiates. Hughes went on to elucidate the chemical structures of these molecules and showed them to be pentapeptides (molecules comprising a chain of five amino acids).

He christened them met-enkephalin and leu-enkephalin after the names of the terminal amino acids (methionine and leucine respectively). The discovery of these two endogenous opiates was merely the tip of the iceberg, and they were soon joined by a range of other more complex molecules which fell into two broad families termed endorphins and dynorphins, all of which were polypeptides (small proteins), and more recently the endomorphins, which are tetrapeptides. Thirty years later we still do not know the precise role of these mammalian opiates, although it is clear that they do act as endogenous painkillers. They probably play a role as mediators of that sense of well-being associated with exercise or the consumption of certain foods like chocolate.

All of the plant-derived opiates and these endogenous polypeptides bind to so-called opiate receptors in the brain, gastrointestinal tract and elsewhere. The most important of these are the so-called mu-receptors, which are large proteins on the surface of responsive cells. Attachment of morphine and other opiates to these receptors results in the opening of an ion channel through the nerve cell membrane. This allows an outpouring of potassium ions which induces inhibition of nerve cell function. The ultimate result is pain prevention. In the gastrointestinal tract, binding of opiates to nerve cells has the effect of slowing peristalsis and leading to constipation.

The mechanisms by which opiates induce euphoria and a feeling of tranquillity are not known, though there is some evidence that in certain parts of the brain they enhance the release of the nerve signalling molecule (neurotransmitter) dopamine, which is intimately involved with the pleasure responses.

There has been a recent surge in media interest in what is known as Diviner's Sage, correct plant name *Salvia divinorum*, and following the revelation that its major psychoactive component - so called salvinorin A - seems to interact at protein receptors for opiates and dopamine. The plant has long been used by the shamans of the Mazatec culture in Mexico as an aid to spiritual healing and for communing with the gods. It may also have been one of the Aztec's most prized magical preparations, *pipiltzintzintli*, but this is impossible to prove. At present it is not a banned commodity and the plant and its leaves are widely available on the Internet. The dried leaves are usually smoked in a pipe and most users report hilarity and distortions of motion accompanied by visions and altered perception. However, although the onset of these changes is rapid (1-5 minutes), the psychoactive experience only last for 5-10 minutes. So although there has been much talk in the press about comparisons with LSD, there is really little similarity, since LSD exerts its effects over an 8-12 hour period and at about one tenth of the dose.

Over the years there has been intense interest in the chemical synthesis of structural analogues of both morphine and the endogenous opiates. Drugs like etorphine (1000 times more potent than morphine and so potent it is used to immobilise elephants and polar bears) and buprenorphine (25 - 50 times more potent than morphine as an analgesic, but with less potential to cause addiction) are but two examples of very useful analgesics that arose from these studies. Both of these are more lipophilic (easily absorbed into fat) than morphine and therefore cross the blood-brain barrier more easily.

Drugs were developed to counter the effects of morphine, for use in the treatment of overdose and addiction. Naloxone and naltrexone are two highly successful examples of this type of drug. Both work by attaching themselves to sites in the brain and elsewhere where morphine and heroin bind, and either displacing the drug (in overdose) or substituting for it without giving any reward.

All these drugs have more complex structures than morphine, so attempts were made to simplify them. One of the most useful results of this is the drug meperidine (pethidine), with 20% the activity of morphine. It was shown to have opiate-like activity in 1939, and was then marketed as a non-addictive alternative to morphine for treatment of moderate pain. In the event, pethidine produces a similar spectrum of undesirable side-effects to morphine, but its rapid onset of activity and short duration of action make it an especially useful drug for treatment of pain during childbirth.

The structurally-similar methadone is the mainstay of drug rehabilitation. It has similar activity to morphine but with less severe side-effects. It is however addictive, so it can only work when the addict has a serious desire to be weaned off opiates rather than swapping one dependency for another.

Finally, one drug that will be familiar to all those who travel in tropical countries or who frequent kebab vans is loperamide or Imodium. This analogue of methadone acts at opiate receptors in the gut and acts as a very effective anti-diarrhoeal agent – it is 40 to 50 times more effective than morphine and has low penetration of the central nervous system.

We are now pretty well equipped with our armoury of synthetic opiates to deal with pain, addiction and overdose, but the abuse of morphine and in particular heroin goes on with no sign of diminishing. The list of musicians who have paid the price of addiction or overdose is very long. The early jazz musicians of the 1930s were notorious for their heroin habits and famous addicts included Charlie 'Bird' Parker, Chet Baker, Art Pepper and Stan Getz, with Billie Holliday the most famous of the female addicts. Among the pop stars who have been addicted are Ginger Baker and Eric Clapton of Cream, Boy George, Keith Richards of the Rolling

Stones, Pete Townsend of the Who and Marianne Faithfull, while heroin contributed to the deaths of Janis Joplin, Jim Morrison of the Doors, Jerry Garcia of the Grateful Dead, Sid Vicious of the Sex Pistols, Keith Moon of the Who, Jimi Hendrix and many lesser stars.

The association of drug use with the music fraternity will last as long as songs like Bob Dylan's *Rainy Day Women* with its chorus everyone must get stoned, or Procul Harum's *Whiter Shade of Pale* (whose lyrics still defy interpretation) retain their popularity. However, these are but modern variants of the rather weird outpouring of the lesser known Victorian poet Arthur Symons in his the *Opium Smoker*:

> *I am engulfed, and drown deliciously.*
> *Soft music like a perfume, and sweet light,*
> *Golden with audible odours exquisite.*
> *Swathe me with cerements for eternity*
> *Time is no more, I pause and yet I flee,*
> *A million ages wrap me round with night.*
> *I drain a million ages of delight,*
> *I hold the future in my memory.*

CHAPTER FIVE

COCA & COLUMBIAN

Cocaine

The origins of the *acullico* or *'chew'* of coca are lost in the mists of South American history. There are illustrations on Mochican pottery from around 500 AD in what is known as the Classic Epoch of civilisation along the northern coast of Peru, and these depict people with cheek bulges that probably represent a quid of chewed coca. This practice of taking leaves of the coca plant *Erythroxylon coca* (a bushy shrub that grows to a height of 1 to 2 metres), chewing them into a ball and then applying lime or a similar alkali to release the cocaine is thus at least 1500 years old. The first published account of this practice by a European was probably in a letter written by Amerigo Vespucci in 1499. He had landed on the island of Santa Margarita off the northern coast of Venezuela and described how the natives 'all had their cheeks swollen out with a green shrub inside, which they were constantly chewing like beasts'.

It was the Inca empire that elevated the use of coca to an almost divine status. The founding fathers of this empire probably settled near Cusco in what is now Peru around the 12th century, and by the 16th century the empire included nearly a million square miles of country that stretched all the way from present-day Ecuador in the north to central Chile in the south. It encompassed all of what is now Ecuador,

Peru, Bolivia, and parts of Chile, Colombia and Argentina – an empire that rivalled in extent that of the Romans. Like the Roman Empire the Inca Empire was criss-crossed by an excellent road network.

This was a totalitarian régime with no written language and without wheeled transport, where human sacrifice was a common occurrence, and in which *Erythroxylon coca* was a sacred plant – a living manifestation of divine beings – and as such was used mainly by the nobility. Louis Lewin in his *Phantastica: Narcotic and Stimulating Drugs* cites an Indian legend that claimed the gods had presented Man with the coca plant to *satisfy the hungry, provide the weary and fainting with new vigour, and cause the unhappy to forget their miseries.* A more recreational use was claimed by William Mortimer in his *Divine Plant of the Incas: History of Coca* (1901), in which he described an initiation ceremony for young Inca men of the noble class (the *huaraca*) in which they competed in races and other feats of athleticism while maidens offered them coca and chicha beer while crying 'come quickly youths, for we are waiting', an offer that would have been hard to refuse even without the cocaine and alcohol!

The arrival of the *conquistadores* at the heart of the Inca empire in 1532, with their horses, wheeled transport and firearms, must have been a terrifying experience. None the less the Inca people held out until 1572, though they were subjected to huge loss of life from war and imported diseases (smallpox, measles and influenza). It is estimated that the total Inca population of perhaps 16 million was reduced by 60-90% following the Spanish invasion.

The Spaniards were not slow to notice the benefits of coca consumption, which included appetite suppression as well as the alleviation of thirst and fatigue and the sensation of cold. So while coca consumption had primarily been reserved for the Inca nobility, the invaders now used the drug to extend the working day of the Inca slaves who worked the gold, silver and tin mines on a near-starvation diet. Based on harvest records, it has been estimated that annual consumption of coca leaves during the three centuries of the Spanish domination of Peru and Bolivia was probably around six million kilograms. During this period vast quantities of silver and gold were exported to Spain, but the cost to the native population was severe.

So what about the present-day situation for the *coquero*? Coca chewing is still very much part of Peruvian culture, with daily consumption of around 10-100 grams of leaves, producing up to 300mg of cocaine extracted into the saliva. From a population of nearly 30 million in Peru, as many as three million chew coca, with perhaps as many as 15 million users throughout South America. Coca is a constituent of such everyday items as chewing gum and toothpaste, and is present in a tea known as *maté de coca*. The relief of fatigue, especially at high altitude, is clearly beneficial, though the symptoms of prolonged use include a pallid complexion, muscular weakness and apathy. This may be due to malnutrition and overgrowth of the liver, though various claims have been made for the nutritional qualities of coca leaves (50-70% of which are usually swallowed), including suggestions that *coqueros* have increased longevity.

John Lloyd in his *Treatise on Coca* (1913) provided one of the first modern accounts of the effects of coca consumption:

After eating a simple breakfast of ground corn porridge they (Colombian Indians in this case) *would start with their heavy packs, weighing from seventy-five to more than one hundred pounds, strapped to their backs. All day long they travelled at a rapid gait, over steep mountain spurs and across mucky swamps, at an altitude, that to us, without any load whatever, was most exhausting. On these trips these Indians neither rested anywhere nor ate at noon, but incessantly sucked their wads of coca throughout the entire day.*

An earlier observer, the Portuguese explorer Hipolito Unanue, noted a further property of coca in his *Disertacion sobre el aspecto, cultivo, commercio, y virtudes de la famosa planta del Peru nombrada coca* (1794):

Certain coqueros, 80 years of age and over, and yet capable of such prowess (with women) as young men in the prime of life would be proud of.

What is clear is that consumption of coca helped to maintain the new Spanish colonies. As the administrator Juan Matienzo de Peralta noted in 1561, 'If there was no coca there would be no Peru'. However, the clergy of the cathedral of Cusco, while deriving considerable revenues from the sale of coca, none the less denounced addiction to the drug.

Knowledge of the properties of coca leaves had reached Europe by the sixteenth century, and the tales of the various explorers like the Frenchman Charles Marie de la Condamine (who was one of the first to report the native uses of rubber, quinine and curare) and the German Alexander von Humboldt (who amongst many things reported on the use of hallucinogenic snuffs) excited the imagination of European society. At one point the *Gentleman's Magazine* of 1814 contained an editorial urging Sir Humphry Davy (as one of England's top scientists) to turn his attentions to experimentation with coca so that it could be used as a substitute for food, allowing people to go without eating if the mood took them.

The Italian Paolo Mantegazza did much to enhance awareness of coca's properties in the 19th century. He was born in Monza in 1831, and after training as a doctor spent several years practising in the Argentine Republic and Paraguay. He observed the use of coca in Peru and in 1859 tried it himself, writing of these experiences in his book *Sulle Virtu Igieniche e Medicinali delle Coca*. He considered coca to be a miracle drug that might help change mankind.

However it was the introduction of Vin Mariani in 1863 that first brought coca to the European consumer. Angelo Mariani was born in Corsica in 1838 and trained to be a chemist. He certainly knew of the writings of Mantegazza, and put this knowledge to good use with the invention of Vin Mariani, which was prepared by steeping coca leaves in Bordeaux wine. This was a major commercial success throughout Europe, selling under the slogan 'fortifies and refreshes body and brain'.

The alcoholic extract of the coca leaves was also served up in the form of Paté Mariani and Pastilles Mariani, and the success of these preparations was as much due to the vigorous advertising campaign mounted by Mariani as to its efficacy. Mariani supplied free samples of his product to many of the famous figures of the time, requesting a small written contribution in return. Their responses included short biographies, essays, sketches and pieces of music. H G Wells, Jules Verne, Alexandre Dumas, August Rodin, Gabriel Fauré and Emile Zola all responded, and the contributions from these satisfied customers were collected by Mariani over a period of years and published in the form of a thirteen-volume portfolio entitled *Figures Contemporaines*.

The British Library in London has a complete set of these books, and the testimonials are charming. Dumas wrote *'le vin c'est le santé'* (wine is health). Zola claimed that Vin Mariani was *la liqueur de vie qui allait combattre la débilité humaine* (the liquor of life which combats human debilities). Fauré sent an eight bar composition, Rodin drew a sketch and Jules Verne claimed that even one bottle of the extraordinary Vin Mariani was sufficient to ensure 100 years of life. Pope Leo XIII is also alleged to have never been without a hip flask containing Vin Mariani, and awarded Mariani the Vatican gold medal for his product.

These relatively crude extracts of coca were soon superseded by something purer and more potent. In 1853, the German pharmacist Heinrich Wackenroder had isolated a crude greenish extract from coca leaves using a mixture of alcohol and water. Seven years later, Albert Niemann of Göttingen, using Wackenroder's method of extraction, managed to obtain crystals which he christened cocaine. He managed to carry out preliminary structural investigations and also studied some simple chemical manipulations of the aqueous solution of his crystals. He reported:

Its solutions have an alkaline reaction, a bitter taste, promote the flow of saliva and leave a peculiar numbness, followed by a sense of cold when applied to the tongue.

It was this report that probably attracted Sigmund Freud to begin his studies with cocaine, though he was also an admirer of the works of Mantegazza. His subsequent enthusiasm was revealed in his review article about contemporary research on cocaine entitled '*über Coca*' and published in 1884:

A few minutes after taking cocaine, one experiences a certain exhilaration and feeling of lightness. One feels a certain furriness on the lips and palate, followed by a feeling of warmth in the same areas.

It seems Freud was also inspired to use cocaine for amorous purposes. In a letter to his fiancée Martha Bernays he wrote:

Woe to you my princess when I come. I will kiss you red and feed you until you are plump. And if you are forward, you shall see who is the stronger, a gentle little girl who doesn't eat enough or a big wild man who has cocaine in his body.

He was also impressed by the apparent lack of ill effects and by reports from the eminent toxicologist Sir Robert Christison of his great feats of mountain climbing at the age of 78 and under the influence of coca.

Long intensive physical work is performed without any fatigue… this result is enjoyed without any of the unpleasant after-effects that follow exhilaration brought about by alcohol… absolutely no craving for further use of cocaine appears after use.

Freud's unbridled enthusiasm led him to recommend the injection of cocaine as a cure for morphine addiction, which was of course a disaster. He was not alone in giving this dangerous advice, since there had been a number of reports from the US which also suggested the value of cocaine in morphine addiction. Freud's well-documented attempts to help his friend Ernst von Fleischl-Marxow overcome his morphine addiction, which had been acquired following use of the drug for treatment of severe pain associated with an amputation, led to the poor man becoming dependent upon both drugs.

On a more positive note Freud listed a number of other therapeutic uses of cocaine, which included treatment of digestive disorders ('I have learned to spare myself stomach troubles by adding a small amount of cocaine to salicylate of soda', he wrote), and use of the drug for asthma, weight loss due to mercury treatment and as an aphrodisiac.

Of more lasting value were Freud's instructions to his assistant Carl Koller, a house surgeon at the Vienna General Hospital, to try to exploit the pain-killing properties of cocaine. In the event, Koller demonstrated in 1884 the potent anaesthetic properties of the drug. He and a colleague experimented first with frogs, then with a rabbit and a dog, touching the corneas of their eyes with the blunt end of a needle after instillation of a cocaine solution. They observed no apparent sensation of pain or discomfort. Emboldened by these results, they instilled a solution of cocaine under their own eyelids before touching their corneas with a pinhead. Koller later reported:

We could make a dent in the cornea without the slightest awareness of touch, let alone any unpleasant sensation or reaction. With that, the discovery of local anaesthesia was completed.

The potential of the drug, not only in ophthalmology but also in general surgery, was realised immediately, and the editorial in the *British Medical Journal* of 2nd November 1884 captured the excitement of the time:

Hydrochlorate of cocaine is at the present moment attracting an amount of attention rarely accorded to any therapeutic agent not of the very first rank. It may be fairly said that the news of the introduction of a new local anaesthetic has been hailed with universal satisfaction.

This led to a flurry of interest and activity in the pharmaceutical industry. The production of cocaine by the German company Merck increased from less than one kilogramme in 1883 to more than 8000 kilograms in 1885. Supplies for Great Britain were obtained from coca plants that had been introduced into Ceylon in the 1880s, and there were also Dutch plantations and factories in Indonesia, especially in Java.

Across the Atlantic in Georgia, coca was about to become a household name for another reason. John Stith Pemberton was born in Knoxville, Georgia in 1831, and after early schooling trained to be a pharmacist. By the outbreak of the Civil War in 1861 he had established a thriving wholesale business specialising in natural remedies, but left this to serve with distinction in the Confederate Army, and was seriously wounded in a battle near Columbus, Georgia in 1865. This wartime trauma and probable addiction to opium was followed by post-war bankruptcy that left him determined to make his mark in business, and this he did with huge success when he introduced Pemberton's French Wine Coca in the early 1880s. He freely admitted that this was based on Vin Mariani but claimed that his product was superior in its effects as an *ideal nerve tonic, health restorer and stimulant* – or so the advertisements proclaimed.

Initially his drink contained coca leaf extract, kola nut extract and wine, but following the imposition of prohibition in Georgia in 1886, the wine was replaced with sugar syrup. This new beverage was, Pemberton claimed:

A direct tonic to the nerves and muscles, and acts so happily on the brain that laborious thinkers and students who have used it have given it the name of 'intellectual beverage'.

In a more fanciful claim, Pemberton tried to enhance its appeal even further:

Coca is a most wonderful invigorator of the sexual organs and will cure seminal weakness, impotence etc when all other remedies fail.

Heady stuff, in America's Bible Belt. Searching around for a more commercial name, Pemberton called his beverage 'Coca-Cola' and made his fortune. The name, however, was almost lost in 1904 when the US Government became alarmed about the addictive properties of cocaine and forced the manufacturers to remove the extracts of coca. They also tried to make the Coca-Cola Company change the name, but after extensive legal wrangling the company won the day, the courts ruling that the names Coca-Cola and 'Coke' had become part of the American language and to ban them would be seen as inappropriate use of government powers.

The first cocaine 'epidemic' in the US probably started around 1880 and ran until the 1930s. For much of this time cocaine was readily available from pharmacists and also found its way into a large number of patent medicines with the cocaine content ranging from around 1% to a staggering 35%, in Agnew's Catarrh Powder. There were even 'cocaine parlors'. As the abuse of the drug grew in scale, the need for legislation became urgent. Initially the Pure Food and Drug Act of 1906 legislated for the removal of cocaine (and other supposed poisons) from patent medicines, then the passing of the Harrison Narcotic Act in 1914 identified the dangerous nature of the drug. However, many US states had by then introduced their own legislation curtailing the sale of a drug that became increasingly associated with crime, especially criminal acts carried out by what the newspapers described as 'cocaine-crazed negroes'.

In the UK, the Dangerous Drugs Act of 1920 eliminated easy access to cocaine and other drugs, though they had earlier (in 1916) been denied to serving members of the armed forces as part of the Defence of the Realm Act. The drug was still readily available (at a price) in London and the other major cities, not least because there was a huge number of unlicensed dentists who had a legitimate need for it. Around the world most countries introduced controlling legislation and by the 1930s the first 'epidemic' of cocaine use was over. Increasingly drug users turned to cheaper alternatives like the amphetamines. The second wave of cocaine abuse began in association with the new freedoms and evanescent pop culture of the 1960s.

For much of the 20th century cocaine hydrochloride was administered by snorting or sniffing (the scientific term is insufflation), producing an immediate 'rush' and an optimum effect in about 10-15 minutes. The cocaine salts were easy to produce and involved maceration of the coca leaves in a dilute solution of hydrochloric acid, followed by separation of the leaf mass and evaporation of the water to produce an off-white residue. In this way 1 kg of cocaine hydrochloride of purity 40-65% could be obtained from 100 kg of leaves.

Sniffing a 'line of coke' has usually been effected using a rolled bank note, a straw, a pen casing, or even a tampon applicator. However, regular use of cocaine salts by this route of administration inevitably leads to rhinitis and eventual destruction of the nasal septum. In the early 1970s, so called 'free-basing' started to replace cocaine hydrochloride snorting. The free base was produced by neutralising the acid moiety (sulphate or hydrochloride) using a weak base, such as ammonia or sodium bicarbonate, to provide an off-white precipitate of cocaine which could be separated by filtration or extracted into diethyl ether. This was then melted and the fumes were inhaled via a water pipe. This led to a more intense and rapid neural response, since the large surface area of the lungs ensured efficient access to the blood stream and then the brain.

Soon after, in 1983, 'crack' cocaine became freely available. This was prepared by simply mixing cocaine salts and sodium bicarbonate in water, then evaporating the water to produce a rock-like mass of cocaine, which was then smoked. The crackling sound emanating from the hot residue inspired the name 'crack' cocaine. Smoking crack cocaine induces an effect within 4-6 seconds, described as the 'cocaine rush' and usually associated with euphoria and pleasure compared to the best sexual experiences. Both these new types of cocaine led to rapid dependence

Such dependence on cocaine obviously required a plentiful supply of the drug, and the drug barons of South America were very happy to oblige. It has been estimated that between 1970 and the late 1980s the annual coca harvest (the new leaves can be collected as often as four times per year) in Peru and Bolivia rose from 30,000 tons to nearly 400,000 tons.

Coca leaves are usually dried in the sun, then chopped (often with a strimmer), before being placed in a large drum and covered with kerosene or other solvent. After several hours of extraction, the kerosene is siphoned off and cocaine is extracted into dilute sulphuric acid solution. Relatively pure cocaine can then be precipitated by careful neutralisation. The resultant paste or *pasta* is then generally passed on to Colombia for processing into pure cocaine or its hydrochloride salt.

In the 70s and 80s this was then sent to the Caribbean or the Bahamas for onward shipment by fast boat or light plane to Florida, but these days it is often exported to West Africa for onwards transmission. By the early 1980s as many as 80 planes were making drugs drops over Florida every night, fuelling the new yuppie cocaine culture that was sweeping most US cities. At this time around 75% of the cocaine used in the USA originated in Colombia.

A manifestation of the enthusiasm for this new 'cocaine epidemic' was the appearance of a host of expensive insufflation aids like gold-plated straws and razor blades, which became the new 'must-have' accessories. In 1981, President Ronald Reagan and Vice President George Bush (senior) officially launched their War on Drugs, directed at the South American cartels. Initially the US targeted the Florida route of importation, so the cartels switched to a new route via Mexico. By 1994 the revenues being earned by the criminal gangs in Mexico exceeded $30 billion, which dwarfed the country's oil exports of less than $10 billion.

During the 70s and 80s, one man dominated the trafficking of drugs from Colombia - Pablo Escobar, head of the Medellín cartel. He was born in a suburb of Medellín in December 1949, and after an early career in petty street crime (stealing cars and protection rackets), he graduated to become one of the most murderous and successful drug dealers in South American history.

An early brush with law enforcement agents in 1976 provided a cogent signal of how Escobar proposed to operate. He was arrested in possession of about 40 kg of cocaine, but this did not lead to a conviction because the arresting officers and the judge who sent him for trial were all murdered soon after his arrest. His operations were so successful that by the mid 1980s he was claimed to be making $1 million per day from his activities. The South American cocaine business was reputed to have had a larger annual income than giant American corporations like Boeing and Proctor and Gamble.

Not surprisingly Escobar allowed himself a lavish lifestyle at his luxury ranch, which had its own airstrip, but he also liked to think of himself as a South American Robin Hood, building homes for the poor and providing them with food, medical supplies and sports facilities. He was absolutely ruthless in pursuing a policy that was usually described as *plata o plomo*, that is silver (for bribes) or lead (bullets) where bribes were not accepted.

Campaigning anti-drugs politicians and police chiefs did not usually survive for very long. The Justice Minister, Rodrigo Lara Bonilla, was particularly assiduous in his pursuit of Escobar. In March 1984 he masterminded raids on several of Escobar's processing operations, seizing more than 8000 kg of high purity cocaine worth about $1 billion in the USA. However, even Bonilla's luck eventually ran out when one of Escobar's assassination squads caught up with him in rush-hour traffic in Bogotà later that month and ended his brief career.

This assassination of a popular politician precipitated an outpouring of popular revulsion in both Colombia and the USA, and the Colombian Government was forced into wide-ranging anti-drugs activities. Unfortunately this simply incensed Escobar, and a near civil-war situation existed for much of the rest of the decade, with Escobar's henchmen bombing and murdering politicians, judges and the police with apparent impunity. They also fought a running battle with the increasingly powerful Cali cartel, their main Colombian competitors. On March 25th 1989, Escobar's henchmen were responsible for a synchronised bombing campaign in Cali, Medellín and Bogotà aimed at policemen, politicians and rival cartel operatives. Inevitably there were numerous civilian casualties as well.

By September 1990 the Government (and the people of Colombia) had suffered enough and an amnesty was declared. The deal stipulated that if Escobar and the other drug cartel members gave themselves up, they would receive lenient treatment, and most importantly would not face deportation to the USA where the CIA was desperate to get its hands on them. In the event, Escobar surrendered in June 1991 and was then incarcerated along with his henchmen in a luxurious prison (appropriately called *la Catedral*) of his own design, which included a gym and chalet accommodation for visiting (female) visitors. He was even allowed out to watch local football matches and for shopping expeditions.

In prison he carried on business as usual, including organisation of the cocaine trade and contract killing. Eventually the Government could take no more and they sought to move him to one of their own less salubrious gaols, but Escobar fled from his own prison in July 1992 and went on the run in and around Medellín. The Cali cartel now helpfully set up a group of vigilantes – los PEPES (*Perseguidos por Pablo Escobar*) – to hunt him down with a tempting reward of $5 million attached. Escobar's friends and associates, especially his many lawyers, were rapidly eliminated. From November 1993 the Government began to use Escobar's wife and children as the bait for their trap, and the net began to close around Escobar himself.

The events surrounding his eventual capture and death are still the subject of folklore, but probably involved a team that included special forces from both the US and Colombian armies with sophisticated communications equipment. What is clear is that he was located because he was careless with his use of a radiophone, and he died in a shoot-out (or was assassinated or even committed suicide

– he received at least one bullet to the head) on December 2nd 1993, and the Medellín Cartel promptly folded in his absence. But as with most drug operations, there were others waiting to step into the breach and there is little sign in 2012 that the flow of cocaine from Colombia and Mexico to the USA has been halted.

The Cali cartel certainly became a major new force, not only for cocaine but increasingly for the growing Colombian opium industry. The cartel had always been a little more subtle in its methods than the Medellín cartel. They bought their enemies rather than killing them, and at one point in the mid-1990s they allegedly controlled one third of the Colombian Congress. Their distribution networks also had greater sophistication. Small groups (cells) of distributors operated in most big US cities, avoiding detection by using a large number of mobile phones which were discarded after just a few calls. A code of silence was also enforced through a campaign of threats against the families of the traffickers. By the turn of the century, the Colombian Government claimed to have imprisoned most of the Cali cartel members, though as much as 80% of the world's cocaine still originates in Colombia.

Another 'star' of the cocaine trade was Manuel Noriega, born in Panama in 1934. Brought up under poor circumstances by foster parents, he received most of his education in military academies in Peru and the USA. By 1981 he was head of the Panamanian armed forces and effectively controlling the country, presidents not withstanding.

Noriega was undoubtedly supported at this time by the CIA. This power base allowed him essentially complete control over the export of Colombian cocaine across the Panamanian border and domination of a money-laundering service for the drugs money flowing back. He also sanctioned the construction of a huge cocaine-processing factory for the Medellín cartel in the Darien jungle just inside Panama. The

CIA had been active in Colombia since the 1960s. It is not clear whether their activities extended to supporting the vast drug-trafficking operations of the Contras, but either way a large quantity of American arms and equipment passed to the Contras via Panama with Noriega's help. However, when the extent of Noriega's involvement in the cocaine trade became apparent, a US invasion force of 24,000 service personnel was sent to Panama City in December 1989 to arrest him.

The story now enters the realms of farce, since Noriega sought refuge within the Papal Nuncio and was prised from it only after the American forces bombarded the building with non-stop and very loud pop music for several days. This military adventure cost the lives of 23 American servicemen and hundreds of innocent residents of Panama City.

Noriega was subsequently tried in the US, convicted of various offences of drug trafficking, money laundering etc and kept in prison until 2007. In 2010 he was extradited to France to stand trial for money laundering, and although convicted he was extradited one more time to Panama, where he had already been tried in his absence for murder. Since late 2011 he has been serving a 20-year sentence for this crime, so he has well and truly been punished for his many drug-related crimes.

Funding for the various US operations in Central America was initially approved by Congress as part of the War on Drugs, but this august body later got cold feet when they appreciated that US-backed forces were trying to overthrow a legally-elected government in Nicaragua. In order to make good the shortfall in funding, the CIA appointed Colonel Oliver North, who had served with distinction in the Marine Corps in Vietnam, to take charge of fund-raising for the Contras. This he did by selling TOW anti-tank missiles to Iran and ploughing back the profits into the Contra activities. The shooting down (by the Sandinistas) in October 1986 of a C-123 transport plane loaded with arms and incriminating documents, not to mention three American crewmen, opened the floodgates of revelations about the Iran-Contra connection and led eventually to Senator John Kerry's so-called Irangate investigation. Almost inevitably, clear evidence of Contra involvement in cocaine smuggling emerged, and although CIA involvement in these activities was never established, the whole sorry affair provides yet another example of America's unhappy experiences with the shady organisations it has supported, not to mention the countries like Iran that ended up on its black list (Axis of Evil). Kerry's committee concluded in its report of April 1989:

In the name of helping the Contras… .the credibility of governmental institutions has been jeopardised by the Administration's decision to turn a blind eye to domestic and foreign corruption associated with the international narcotics' trade.

Interestingly, Oliver North was eventually cleared of all charges due to certain procedural irregularities, and he has since carved out a successful career for himself on television and as an author. His latest book, published in May 2008, was entitled *American Heroes*, and contains, among other things, his views on fighting global terrorism!

From the early 1990s, the American military became more involved in what was termed Plan Colombia, which involved funding for military intervention and aid in the ratio of about 9:1. A programme of defoliation commenced in Peru and Bolivia. This had the effect of shifting coca production to Colombia, where the area under cultivation increased from 120,000 hectares in 1999 to more than 170,000 hectares in 2001. At this point the defoliation campaign switched to Colombia.

Despite these major military campaigns, the street price of cocaine has continued to fall, and the typical cost in the USA is now a mere 20% of what is was in real terms in the 1980s. Little surprise that there are at least 6 million users of cocaine in the USA, to add to half a million users of heroin and more than 25 million users of marijuana. Certainly there is little evidence to suggest that the campaign launched by Nancy and Ronald Reagan in 1986 has had much effect. They famously exhorted youth to 'Just say Yes to your life, and when it comes to alcohol and drugs, just say No'.

In the UK the problem has never been so serious, though the relentless campaign waged by the Thatcher government in the1980s probably drove the criminal gangs into becoming more efficient and professional. She famously warned them 'We are after you. The pursuit will be relentless. We shall make your life not worth living'. But it is certain that many of the drugs barons have outlasted her time in office, and there was never a shortage of cocaine for the City yuppies of the 1980s and 90s.

There is a very extensive literature on cocaine use and abuse, and a good selection of modern writing on the subject of abuse and addiction is contained within the pages of *White Lines* by Stephen Hyde and Geno Zanetti. This contains extracts from the writings of among others Aleister Crowley, William Burroughs, Miles Davis, Carrie Fisher, Stephen King, Will Self, J G Ballard and Irvine Welsh. In the main the extracts make very depressing reading. Aleister Crowley is the exception. He extolled the aphrodisiac virtues of cocaine as follows:

I had never been particularly keen on women… but with cocaine things are absolutely different. Until you've got your mouth full of cocaine, you don't know what kissing is. One kiss goes on from phase to phase and you never get tired… you're on full speed all the time. (from Diary of a Drug Fiend)

The excesses of Hollywood in the yuppie 1980s are eloquently described by Charles Fleming:

Avoiding narcotics in Hollywood in the 1980s was as difficult as avoiding the Southern California sun. Drugs were everywhere, and cocaine was king, the champagne of the recreational stimulants... The social uses of cocaine were myriad: it was a terrific icebreaker, an instant pick-me-up and a great come-on. Everything went better with coke. It stimulated conversation and intellectual activity, and increased sexual appetite and prowess. It didn't leave telltale odours or next-day hangovers. It wasn't passé, like marijuana or martinis, and it wasn't deadly like heroin. It was portable and easy to hide. Ingesting it required no 'kit', no special equipment. And, as an added bonus, it was just expensive enough that the hoi polloi couldn't afford it.

An excellent account of the activities of a 1970s cocaine smuggler is provided in the novel *Snowblind* by Robert Sabbag, which contains an often hilarious account of the brief career of Zachary Swan, an alias for a real and very successful coke runner. The style of the writing owes much to the hippy culture of the time, but a short extract will give something of the flavour of the book, as well as an idea of the excesses that were very often the norm. Here Swan describes how he and his friends use some of the half-kilo of cocaine that he has just received from Colombia hidden in a carved wooden tribal head:

The skull yielded up 500 grams of high grade uncut cocaine, double wrapped in clear plastic... and the coke was (soon) performing fabulous and outlawed miracles in the heads of Swan, his girlfriend (and two Australian friends). The Bolivian brain food they had ingested was only one course in a sublime international feast which featured French wine,

English gin, Lebanese hashish, Colombian cannabis, and a popular American synthetic known pharmacologically as methaqualone... The party went out of control somewhere in the early hours before dawn, and the steps he had taken to mimimize his losses were eventually undermined by the immutable laws of chemistry – his mind, simply, had turned to soup.

Perhaps the most famous fictional cocaine user was Sherlock Holmes, here describing his habit in *The Sign of Four*:

I suppose that its influence is physically a bad one. I find it, however, so transcendingly stimulating and clarifying to the mind that its second action is a matter of small moment.

There is no evidence that Sir Arthur Conan Doyle ever used cocaine, but interestingly, as part of his training to be a doctor, he spent one year (1890) in Vienna studying ophthalmology. It seems highly probable he heard about the discoveries of Freud and Koller which had been made in that city just six years earlier, and that this inspired him to depict the use of the drug in his books.

A greater mystery surrounds the writing of the *Strange Case of Dr Jekyll and Mr Hyde* by Robert Louis Stevenson in 1885. The first draft of this tale of split personality induced by a drug was apparently written in a frenzied period of six days while Stevenson, who was plagued with lung disease for much of his life, was recovering from a haemorrhage. There is no evidence that he took cocaine, but once again he would have read about the new excitement surrounding the drug, and wanted to describe the split personality of a cocaine addict. The book went on to sell 40,000 copies in the first six months following publication, and by 1901 had sold more than 250,000.

In the 1970s and 80s, the music industry was full of people who admitted using cocaine, often to excess, and famous examples included Marvin Gaye ('blow is what really makes me fly'), Freddie Mercury, Elton John and Phil Spector – whose Christmas card once showed a picture of him snorting coke with the legend 'A little snow at Christmas has never hurt anyone'. Numerous references to cocaine use appear in the lyrics of groups like the Rolling Stones and the Eagles, and the popular 1969 film *Easy Rider*, starring Peter Fonda, Dennis Hopper and Jack Nicholson, with its explicit portrayal of LSD, hashish and cocaine use, did much to establish drug use in popular culture.

So what of the useful medicinal properties of cocaine? In the absence of any firm structural information about the drug, several pharmaceutical companies designed drugs in the latter decades of the 19th century with structures that they believed (correctly as it turned out) to be present within the cocaine molecule. Somewhat surprisingly, several of these companies had good successes, and benzocaine was introduced in 1890 and is still used in throat lozenges. Of more lasting value was procaine (introduced in 1905), which was later given the trade name Novocaine. It dominated the local anaesthetic market until the middle of the 20th century. After 1948 it was largely superseded by lidocaine (Xylocaine), which is now the most widely-used local anaesthetic.

As to the mode of action of cocaine, its anaesthetic effect is caused by a blocking of the so-called sodium channels in nerve cells, eliminating nerve conduction. Its effects on the brain seems to be mainly exerted in the region known as the nuclear accumbens, an area usually associated with pleasurable responses ('reward centre') to stimuli like food and sex. Cocaine attaches to a protein called the dopamine transporter, whose job is to control the reuptake of this nerve signalling molecule (neurotransmitter) into the neurones that release dopamine. As a result of this blockade, dopamine accumulates and the 'reward' response is prolonged and intensified. There are similar though less significant effects on uptake of serotonin (5-HT, another neurotransmitter, mentioned under LSD). Cocaine is reputed to intensify and extend the pleasures of sex (especially orgasm), and most habitual users claim this as one of its most significant effects. The need to take more and more cocaine is usually due to the effects of the 'crash' that occurs after the initial 'cocaine rush' of euphoria. The half-life of cocaine in the blood is only about 50 minutes (the time it takes for half of the cocaine to be broken down), and inhaled cocaine needs replenishment after 10-30 minutes. The overwhelming need to take more coke is nicely summarised by Zachary Swan in Robert Sabbag's *Snowblind*:

And so, at the zenith of the cocaine ecliptic, activity was resumed. What goes up must come down; what comes down must come up. QED. Physics, man. But now, with four people behind some heavy coke, anything was possible.

Chronic use of cocaine can lead to depression and even suicidal tendencies, and this is probably due to changes in the production or sensitivity to dopamine and serotonin. However, a large number of people use cocaine in small amounts occasionally and recreationally, and many would agree with the actress Tallulah Bankhead, who famously claimed 'Cocaine isn't habit forming. I should know I've been using it for years'.

PEACE, POETRY AND POP

Cannabis, hashish, marijuana

When they are harvesting hemp, the workers sometimes experience strange phenomena: the harvester's head is full of whirlwinds or is full of daydreams.

This was the French writer Charles Baudelaire's description in his book *Les Paradis Artificiels* of the effects of harvesting hemp on the harvesters. The whirlwinds and the daydreams were apparently being caused by ingestion (perhaps deliberate) of the mind-expanding constituents from the flower heads of the plant *Cannabis sativa*. Salman Rushdie described a similar intoxication in his novel *Midnight's Children*:

But now the wind changed and began to blow from the north: a cold wind, and also an intoxicating one, because in the north of Kif were the best hashish fields in the land, and at this time of year the female plants were ripe and in heat. The air was filled with the perfume of the heady lust of the plants, and all who breathed in became doped to some extent.

Such exposure to the psychoactive constituents of the plant was nothing new. Hemp seeds have been found in copper vessels associated with Scythian burial sites dating from at least 500-300 BC. Herodotus, writing around 450 BC, talks of a tent-like structure in which the Scythians would use:

A dish placed upon the ground into which they put a number of red hot stones and then add some hempseed... immediately it smokes and gives out such a vapour as no Grecian vapour bath can exceed; the Scythians, delighted, shout for joy.

There is a likely error here since hempseed does not contain any psychoactive constituents, but he was probably confusing the seed with the flower heads or leaves, both of which contain cannabinoids – the psychoactive components of cannabis species. Three distinct species can be identified - *Cannabis sativa*, which is a bushy plant and can grow to a height of 6 metres, and the smaller sub-species *Cannabis indica* and *Cannabis ruderalis*. Recent genetic studies indicate that *Cannabis sativa* probably arose in Kazakhstan, while *Cannabis indica* probably first appeared in the western Himalayas.

Long before the hemp plant was used for mind-expanding activities, various ancient civilisations had discovered the value of hemp fibres from the thick stems of mature cannabis plants for manufacturing cords and ropes, and for cloth and paper making. These activities certainly go back as far as 4000 BC in China and 3000 BC in Turkestan. The seed oil was also valued as a food source, and the medicinal properties of the plant are mentioned in the Shen Nung herbal published in the first century AD, relating to the activities of the great Chinese herbalist Shen Nung who appears to have practised around 2800 BC.

The Zend-Avesta, an ancient Persian religious text from about

600 BC, actually describes an intoxicating resin from hemp, and various historians have wrongly identified this as the soma of ancient Indian culture. Certainly extracts from the cannabis plant known as *bhang* have been used as part of Hindu and Buddhist religious activities for hundreds of years, and as a component of Ayurvedic medicine since at least 1500 BC. The Ebers papyrus from ancient Egypt, which also dates from around 1500 BC, probably mentions hemp (*shemshemet*) for the treatment of pain and fever.

Bhang is just one of many terms used to describe preparations from the plant and refers to ground leaves and flowers, often mixed with milk and spices and gently heated, and then consumed as a beverage or in the form of sweets. The Indians also use another form which contains resin from the trichomes (hair-like projections from various parts of the plant), with mature flowers of female plants providing the richest source of resin. The resin may be collected by scraping the trichomes and then sifting, or through the use of leather aprons worn by the harvesters as they walk through the crop of cannabis. This method of collection of the sticky exudate is similar to the collection of opium after the poppy capsules have been incised and allowed to 'bleed'.

In either case, this resinous form is the most potent form of cannabis. It is known in India as *charas* and more commonly elsewhere as *hashish*, and is taken with food or smoked. Finally, the ground flowering tops and leaves are consumed with food or smoked (often with tobacco); in Africa this is usually known as *ganja* and elsewhere as *marijuana*. This has widely differing potencies depending on the source of the plants and the content of resin from the flower tops.

The use of hashish as a euphoriant was certainly known to the Romans. Galen wrote in AD 160 of hemp cakes that produced a sense of well-being when taken in moderation, and intoxication if taken to excess. In Persia and much of the Middle East hashish was widely used as an alternative to the much-hated alcohol, since its consumption with food did not lead to intoxication which was strictly forbidden in the Koran. Its use is mentioned several times in *The 1001 Arabian Nights*. It was certainly employed as a medicine by the time of the famous Persian physician Rhazes (10th century AD).

Through the centuries claims have been made for the drug's efficacy for conditions ranging from dandruff and dysentery to tuberculosis, leprosy and venereal disease. Success in the treatment of these conditions was probably illusory, though its use as a stupefacient during childbirth and for sleep induction were undoubtedly valid.

Arab traders and invaders are generally believed to have exported the use of hashish into Africa, while their invasion of Spain in the 8th century ensured that the more potent strains of the plant entered Southern Europe. In Northern Europe hemp had been cultivated from about 400 AD for rope and cloth manufacture, and it was used for paper making from the 12th century. In the time of the Tudors it was valued so highly for the manufacture of rigging for naval vessels that both Henry VIII and Elizabeth I issued decrees requiring landowners to set aside a portion of their land for hemp cultivation. Fines were imposed (as much as 5 shillings during Elizabeth's reign) for failure to comply, and for this reason and also because the production process was both tedious and very malodorous, cultivation of hemp became very unpopular.

By the mid 17th century England was obtaining most of its hemp from Russia. None the less, the overwhelming might of the British Navy was at least partly due to the fine rigging on its ships. In Venice, there was a 300-metre long factory for rope making (*corderia*) in the naval base – the Arsenale – and this helped to ensure that the Venetian merchant and naval fleets were the most powerful in the Mediterranean. Hemp was also introduced into North America by the European settlers and into South America by the conquistadores, and in both instances it was used more or less exclusively for rope and cloth making.

The first stories of the plant's use as a euphoriant were brought to Europe by soldiers returning from the Crusades, and hashish was also inextricably linked to the cult of the Hashshashin. These were the fanatical assassins of the 11th and 12th centuries who were initially under the leadership of the warlord Al-Hasan ibn al-Sabah or Aloidin. He ruled over large swathes of Persia, but his main stronghold was the fortress of Alamut in the Elburz Mountains of northern Persia. The chroniclers of the times were very much in awe of this élite band of Islamic terrorists, and numerous fanciful stories were created about their recruitment and maintenance. The fortress of Alamut was rumoured to be a wondrous place, complete with a superb garden containing four fountains that provided wine, milk, honey, or water, and was also well stocked with beautiful women. In short, it was a kind of earthly paradise.

Marco Polo travelled in this region around 1271 and reported some of the stories that he heard in his book entitled *Il Milione*, of which the most quoted edition was published in 1330. Much of his account is now believed to be fanciful and exaggerated, but he does mention the Old Man of the Mountain (*Il Veglio della Montagna*) and the drugs that were used by the hashshashin (*assassini* in Italian). These induced sleep and made the hashshashin dream about Paradise. His conclusion was that hashish had been employed, though it is more likely that opium would have caused these effects. In any event, his stories and those of the returning crusaders brought hashish to the attention of Europeans for the first time.

In northern Europe, widespread use of cannabis as a euphoriant did not begin until the time of the Napoleonic Wars. Napoleon took his army into Egypt in June 1798. Although his land campaign was successful, Nelson discovered the French fleet in Aboukir Bay on August 1st and all but annihilated it, in what is usually known as the Battle of the Nile. This effectively marooned Napoleon and his army in North Africa, where hashish use was widespread, and with limited access to alcohol the troops developed a penchant for the various foods and drinks containing it. When the remnants of a demoralised French army eventually left Egypt in the summer of 1800, they took their new habit and supplies of hashish with them to France.

Experimentation with this new drug spread slowly, since supplies had to be obtained from North Africa or the Middle East. In order to supply the growing market, trade routes from Turkey and the Middle East were established, with shipments by camel train across the Sinai Desert or by ship to Alexandria. This business grew enormously through the 19th century and into the early part of the 20th.

The first written account of hashish use in France was provided by Dr Jacques-Joseph Moreau in 1845. In his book *Du Haschisch et de l'Alienation Mentale*, he described his observations made during travels in Egypt and the Middle East in the period 1837 to 1840 and his subsequent experiments with mentally-ill patients in the Paris area. He provided one of the most detailed descriptions of the potential for hashish to induce euphoria, distortions of time and space, enhanced aural and visual acuity and hallucinations. Perhaps more significantly, he was the initial supplier of hashish to a group of French writers who formed themselves into 'Le Club des Haschischins' from 1844. The hashish was apparently in the form of a green paste (they described it as a *confiture* or *pâté*), containing hashish, butter, and various ground nuts and spices.

The group used a variety of psychoactive drugs and met on a regular basis in a Paris hotel – Hôtel Pimodan - to experiment with these substances and share their experiences. Accounts of these meetings were recorded by the poet Théophile Gautier in a short piece entitled *Le club des haschischins* in 1846 and also in greater detail by the poet Charles Baudelaire in his famous book *Les Paradis Artficiels*.

Théophile Gautier, writing of his first experience of hashish, recorded that he had been given food that was the same as that used by the Assassins, and goes on to confirm it as hashish. It caused a complete transformation in his senses, with water tasting like wine and meat resembling raspberries. He describes the cries of ecstasy from the other members of the Club:

My God I am happy. I am swimming in ecstasy. I am in Paradise. I plunge into chasms of delight!

Charles Baudelaire was much more expansive. He described the preparation of the hashish that they consumed:

The composition of hashish is made from a decoction of Indian cannabis, butter and a small quantity of opium to produce a green paste with a unique smell.

Baudelaire also identified three distinct phases of response to the drug. In the first there was much laughter, hilarity and spatial distortion, while in the second sounds and colours and numbers became mixed up, and frighteningly difficult mathematical puzzles became explicable. The sense of time also disappeared. Finally in the third phase there was a feeling of calm and feelings of love, and artistic awareness took on a unique form. However, at the end of this apparent passionate endorsement of hashish, he drops the bombshell that he really prefers wine: 'Wine exalts the will. Hashish annihilates it. Wine makes you sociable. Hashish is isolating.'

All of this has to be taken with a degree of scepticism since, like the pop stars of later years, Gautier and Baudelaire and the other members of Le Club des Haschischins were consuming a mixture of drugs and probably alcohol as well. Baudelaire at the very least was both an alcoholic and an opium addict, though his death in 1867 aged 46 was blamed on the syphilis he had contracted as a young man. In any event, Le Club did not last long and by 1849 the members had dispersed.

The experiences of the other members – the painter Eugène Delacroix and the writers Gustave Flaubert, Honoré de Balzac and Alexandre Dumas - were not recorded in detail. Dumas does describe the supposed aphrodisiac effects of hashish on one of his characters, Baron Franz d'Epinay, in *the Count of Monte Cristo*. The Baron, as a guest of Sinbad, alias the Count, at his hideaway on the Island of Monte Cristo, was given a green hashish paste to eat and reports the following:

His body seemed to acquire the lightness of some immaterial being, his mind became unimaginably clear and his senses seemed to double their faculties.

He was then overcome with lust for some marble statues:

This lust was almost pain and this voluptuousness almost torture, as he felt the lips of these statues, supple and cold as the coils of a viper, touched his parched mouth.

Elsewhere in the world other writers and poets were also experimenting. In the USA, Fitz Hugh Ludlow, a pastor's son from New York City, took increasing doses of a tincture from *Cannabis indica* for more than 15 years prior to his death in 1870 and wrote of his experiences in *The Hasheesh Eater*, being *Passages from the Life of a Pythagorean*. This seems to have been a blatant attempt to emulate the success of de Quincey's *Memoirs of an Opium Eater*. It is considered to be a very inferior example of the genre, though it did raise awareness in the USA of the psychoactive properties of hashish.

Louisa M. Alcott, author of that archetypal book on American womanhood *Little Women*, also wrote a short story in 1869 entitled *Perilous Play*, which famously begins with one of the female characters declaring: *If someone does not propose a new and interesting amusement, I shall die of ennui.* She is promptly offered some hashish but declines it. One of her male companions does take some and subsequently declares his undying love for one of the other female characters, but it is all done in a totally chaste and romantic fashion. Unsurprisingly, there is no record of Alcott having taken drugs.

In Britain, William Butler Yeats, Oscar Wilde, Aubrey Beardsley and Havelock Ellis formed a clique of drug takers; it is difficult to disentangle the effects on their literary output of hashish from the effects of opium, mescaline and absinthe which they also consumed. The reprobate and heroin addict Aleister Crowley has already been mentioned. His literary output on the subject of hashish was confined to a few essays in which he was mostly disparaging about the drug, preferring the stronger effects of heroin, cocaine and mescaline (though he claimed that it enhanced his sexual performance with both sexes).

Louis Lewin provided his usual accurate and straightforward account (in his *Phantastica*) of his observations, and described how cannabis users proceeded from 'an exhibition of gaiety in which smokers behave in a very childish and stupid manner' to a dream-like state where 'all the thoughts which pass through the brain are lightened by the sun... and the bonds of time and space are broken'.

However, it is the effects of cannabis use on the music scene, especially in the USA, which begins to dominate the social history of this plant from the 1920s. While hemp had been introduced into the Americas by Europeans as a source of fibres for rope and cloth, it was African slaves shipped in to work in the Brazilian sugar plantations and the American cotton fields who first used the plant for its euphoriant properties. In the British West Indies, Indian workers arriving to replace the slaves in the mid 19th century brought their *ganja* habit with them. In Jamaica they laid the foundations for the rise of the Rastafarian movement, which was a culture engendered by pan-Africanism and for which *ganja* was a sacred herb for healing and meditation. This led ultimately to the emergence of reggae music in the 1960s, with star exponents like Bob Marley who rose to prominence in the USA and Europe from 1971. To this day, many smallholdings in Jamaica will have a small plot dedicated to the growth of *Cannabis sativa*.

The use of cannabis spread north through Central America, and by the 1880s it was being widely used in Mexico, both with food and in the form of cigarettes. Here it was usually known as *marihuana* (later marijuana). Inevitably some cannabis leaked across the border into the southern states of the USA, and it became better known following the incursions of Pancho Villa and his raiding parties from 1916. These brigands were known as the 'cockroaches' and were all users of marijuana – hence the term 'roach' for the stub end of a marijuana cigarette. The song *La cucaracha* also dates from this time:

> *The cockroach, the cockroach,*
> *Now he cannot walk,*
> *Because he don't have, because he's lacking*
> *Marijuanha to smoke.*

The surge of marijuana use in cities like New Orleans and Chicago during the 1920s was contemporaneous with the evolution of jazz and blues music, and regular users included such well known performers as Hoagy Carmichael, Fats Waller and Louis Armstrong. The latter claimed:

Marijuana makes you feel good man, makes you forget all the bad things that happen to a negro.

These musicians gravitated towards the big time music scene in New York, and Harlem in particular, during the 1930s where so-called 'tea pads' became the place to find both jazz and marijuana. A marijuana joint could be obtained for as little as 15 to 50 cents and the lyrics of the songs of this period became more and more explicit about their source of inspiration. The 'Reefer Song' by Fats Waller is a particularly good example of what was known as 'viper music':

> *Dreamed about a reefer five feet long.*
> *Mighty Mezz, but not too strong.*
> *You'll be high, but not for long*
> *If you're a viper.*
> *I'm the king of everything.*
> *I've got to be high before I can swing*
> *Light a tea and let it be*
> *If you're a viper.*

'Mezz', 'muggles' and 'tea' were local slang for marijuana joints. The first term was derived from one of the great characters of the 20s and 30s, Milton 'Mezz' Mezzrow, a jazz clarinet and saxophone player who became in turn a bandleader, entrepreneur and supplier of the best Mexican marijuana, initially in Detroit, then in Chicago and New York City. In his autobiography, *Really the Blues*, he reveals that:

During the years when I sold the stuff, I never 'pushed it'… I sold it to grown-up friends of mine… overnight I was the most popular man in Harlem.

Of course these musical activities, enlivened by marijuana and to a degree cocaine and opium too, did not escape the attention of the media. The newspapers of William Randolph Hearst were particularly vehement in the 1930s in their condemnation of the 'evil weed' and the blacks and Mexicans who used it or peddled it. The government were not slow to act, and in 1937 Roosevelt signed the Marihuana Tax Act. This was a strange piece of legislation, since it sought to raise revenue rather than criminalising the drug. Every time marijuana changed hands a tax of $100 per ounce had to be paid, and in consequence all those who produced or sold the drug had to be registered. The very open use of marijuana was probably reduced by the Act, but more significantly it had the (apparently) unexpected effect of killing off the farming of hemp, and this was to have serious consequences when America needed rope during World War II.

Another effect on marijuana use was the appearance of amphetamines, initially benzedrine and dexedrine and later methedrine (speed), a class of drugs that were cheap and very readily available.

The musicians were not the only ones to gain notoriety from their drug use. Following WWII, the so-called Beat Generation emerged from New York City, led by the likes of Allen Ginsberg, William Burroughs and Jack Kerouac. Their literary and other activities were fuelled by a whole medicine cabinet of drugs including morphine, heroin, peyote, cocaine, speed, marijuana and alcohol. Ginsberg is mostly remembered for his political activism (especially against the Vietnam War), and for his explicit poem *Howl*. This was published in 1956 and celebrated the lives of the Beat Generation. It was almost immediately banned for its alleged obscenity. Ginsberg spent much of his time high on marijuana, peyote or opium, studying the works of William Blake and trying to 'expand his mind and free his soul'.

William Burroughs, an inveterate opium addict, has two claims to notoriety: he shot and killed his common-law wife Joan in 1951 by firing a gun at a glass of water she had balanced on her head – he was of course high as a kite at the time; and he wrote the extremely weird book *Naked Lunch*. This was written over a four-year period in Tangier, partly with the help of Ginsberg and Kerouac, and finally published in 1959, immediately becoming the subject of obscenity trials in several states.

Jack Kerouac made his famous road trip with Neal Cassady (a small-time car thief) in 1948, borne along on a wave of alcohol, speed, peyote and marijuana, and his book of the trip, entitled *On the Road*, was first published in 1957. By today's standards the book is quite tame, with its accounts of criss-crossing America in trucks or wildly-driven cars and descriptions of weird individuals they met along the way, together with attempted seductions of (mainly) teenage girls. But in conservative 1950s America it seemed outrageous. There is little explicit description of drug use, though towards the end the main characters (Sal Paradise, aka Kerouac, and Dean Moriarty, aka Cassady) encounter a woman in Northern Mexico who provided them with some home-grown and very potent marijuana:

He proceeded to roll the biggest bomber anybody ever saw. He rolled (using a brown paper bag) what amounted to a tremendous Corona cigar of tea. It was huge.

They then proceeded to the local brothel to dance and use the local girls, and on the way, Sal looked out of the window and saw Mexico as 'some gloriously riddled glittering treasure-box... I saw streams of gold pouring through the sky and right across the tattered roof of the poor old car' The mambo music in the brothel 'Resounded and flared in the golden, mysterious afternoon like sounds you expect to hear on the last day of the world and the Second Coming'.

Neal Cassady took another famous road trip in 1964 when he drove a converted school bus covered in psychedelic art and fitted with powerful speakers from California to New York. This 'magic bus' was the brainchild of Ken Kesey, the author of *One Flew over the Cuckoo's Nest*, and one of the founding members of the Merry Pranksters, who sought to popularize the use of LSD. As the bus travelled across America broadcasting folk rock at full volume, Kesey was on hand at many of its well-publicised stops to supply LSD for experimentation. These exploits formed the basis of the Tom Wolfe novel entitled the *Electric Kool-Aid Acid Test*.

Ginsberg, Burroughs and Kerouac have had a lasting influence on the social history of cannabis and other drugs, and they were the forerunners in the 1950s of what was to be an explosion of music and literature that emerged in the 1960s, much of it influenced by cannabis and other drugs. The Beat Generation spawned the Beatniks. In the USA especially, these bearded folk dressed mostly in black clothes, openly used marijuana and spread the word about its effects.

Of all the musicians and songwriters who contributed to 60s culture – The Beatles, The Rolling Stones, Cream, The Eagles, The Beach Boys, Led Zeppelin and The Who, all of whom undoubtedly used drugs - it was Robert Zimmerman, aka Bob Dylan, who epitomised the evolution of folk music in the last 40 years of the 20th century. He worshipped the folk-singing rebel Woody Guthrie, studied the works of Ginsberg and Kerouac and wrote some of the most (apparently) drug-inspired lyrics of any performer, in songs including *Mr Tambourine Man*, *Like a Rolling Stone* and in particular *Desolation Row*. Dylan has, however, always steadfastly denied taking any drugs apart from marijuana. In his interview for *Playboy*, published in 1966, he was ambiguous to say the least:

I wouldn't advise anybody to use drugs – certainly not the hard drugs. But opium and hash and pot – those things aren't drugs, they just bend your mind a little. I think everybody's mind should be bent once in a while.

At the end of the 60s, a veritable who's who of the folk-rock scene performed at what was probably the biggest musical event of the decade – perhaps of the century – the music festival at Woodstock in upstate New York in August 1969. Close to 500,000 people attended, the great majority using marijuana at the very least, and spent three days listening to some of the greatest bands of the era. One aspect of this 'happening' that was most striking was the almost total lack of any crime or violence, despite the huge number of people in attendance. This contrasts with the alcohol-fuelled problems that are almost inevitably associated with much smaller events in the 21st century.

This period of 'peace and love' that started with the 'summer of love' in San Francisco in 1967 spawned the hippy culture. Bohemian travellers soon moved on from places like Haight-Ashbury and Big Sur in California to Mexico and Morocco, where cannabis was widely available. The Arab occupation of Morocco from the 8th century had led to the introduction of cannabis there, and from around 1800 a major area of cultivation was in the Rif mountains. *Cannabis sativa* became a staple agricultural crop for the Berber people and the product made from flowerheads and tobacco is known locally as *kif*. Successive rulers of Morocco made little effort to control its production, until the newly-independent government of Morocco used its army in 1962 to try to kerb the Berbers' productivity. However, it was beaten back and crop production was unaffected.

The hippies had a lasting effect on Morocco, not only because they effectively took over cities like Tangier. Their quest for ever stronger forms of cannabis led the Berbers to experiment with more effective ways of extracting the resin from the flowerheads, and hashish increasingly displaced *kif* as the extract of choice. The hippies eventually moved on to more exotic locations such as Nepal, India and Afghanistan, and the production of cannabis in each of these countries expanded to meet their needs, though opium production has always been the main activity in Afghanistan.

By the mid 1990s the major producers of hashish were Lebanon (around 20%), Pakistan (30%) and Morocco (35%), with marijuana being exported in large quantities from Colombia, Mexico and Jamaica. The total world production of cannabis in its various forms probably amounted to about 50,000 tons. In all of these countries, peasant farmers could make a good living by growing cannabis as one of their staple crops. In the 1970s the Mexican border was particularly leaky, with marijuana smuggled into California and Texas by car, truck and boat. Much of this was in small amounts brought in by tourists and small-time operators in their private cars, and many Mexican garages specialised in customising cars (door panels, petrol tanks, etc) for the smuggling trade.

Similarly, small-scale imports came into Britain from Morocco via Spain, often concealed in mobile homes and VW caravanettes. Some idea of the scale of these operations and their sheer audacity can be gained from two books, one that celebrates the 1970s activities of the American smuggler Allen Long - *Smokescreen* by Robert Sabbag - and the other an autobiography of the British smuggler Howard Marks, *Mr Nice*. The former flew DC-3s loaded with cannabis from small dirt strips in Colombia into various quiet airports in the USA, and was finally apprehended in 1991 after over 15 years of drug-related activities that included frequent brushes with murderous drug dealers in both Colombia and the US. In return for a guilty plea he received a five-year jail sentence.

Howard Marks used less gung-ho methods for his smuggling, including commercial flights from Pakistan via Shannon (where the

Irish police were less vigilant), and thence by ferry across the Irish Sea to Britain. He also used a sea-going tug sailing from Colombia to the UK before he was apprehended in 1988 and served seven years for his crimes. His many adventures have now been made the subject of a film also entitled *Mr Nice*, released in October 2010 and starring Rhys Ifans.

Needless to say the increasing use of cannabis preparations from the 1920s had attracted the attentions of the legislators, though there was always a sense that cannabis was somehow less dangerous than opium, heroin or cocaine. A major study of marijuana use in New York City was carried out from 1938 to 1944 at the behest of the then mayor, Fiorello La Guardia. This involved participation by the inmates of Riker's Island Penitentiary and certain patients in the Memorial Hospital, and had the full cooperation of the New York Police Department. It was claimed to be a comprehensive study of the scientific and sociological aspects of marijuana use. The final La Guardia report concluded:

From the study as a whole, it is concluded that marijuana is not a drug of addiction comparable to morphine, and that if tolerance is acquired, this is of a very limited degree. Furthermore, those who have been smoking marijuana for a period of years showed no mental or physical deterioration which may be attributed to the drug.

Of course this predated the 1954 report of the British epidemiologists Richard Doll and Richard Peto about the long-term effects of cigarette smoking and more recent reports of the equally damaging effects of cannabis smoke on the lungs. Despite this apparent clean bill of health, law enforcers in the USA were determined to restrict cannabis use, and the Narcotic Control Act of 1956 laid down harsh penalties for possession of heroin, cocaine and marijuana with no discrimination between the three drugs. The Act suggested prison terms of 10, 20 and 40 years for first, second and third offences respectively, with terms of 5-20 years for a first offence of dealing in the drugs. Some US States introduced a mandatory death penalty!

The United Nations introduced its own legislation in 1961, with the Single Convention on Narcotic Drugs, which prohibited the use of all narcotics and marijuana except for medical uses.

In typical fashion, Allen Ginsberg led one of the first lobby groups to campaign for decriminalisation – LeMar or Legalise Marijuana – which he set up in 1964. He became increasingly vocal and his credibility was finally accepted. In the normally staid *Atlantic Monthly* he wrote a strong article in November 1966 in which he declared:

The actual experience of the smoked herb has been completely clouded by a fog of dirty language by the diminishing crowd of fakers who have not had the experience.

This was coming at the same time as Timothy Leary's exhortation to *turn on, tune in, drop out*, together with an increased level of social upheaval in the USA (and elsewhere) associated with the Civil Rights movement, student unrest, the Vietnam War, the rise of feminism, and the general atmosphere of sex, drugs and rock and roll.

A surge in the use of marijuana in the UK began at the end of World War II, most of it smuggled in from Africa or the Middle East. As in the USA, the press began a campaign of fear regarding the evil influence of 'coloured racketeers' peddling the drug to unsuspecting teenage girls. Less seriously, Chapman Pincher in the *Daily Express* promulgated the theory that reefers and rhythm were directly connected via the 'minute brainwaves' of jazz fans, causing their bodies to gyrate in sympathy with the music. In 1965 the Dangerous

Drugs Act placed cannabis and its products in the same category as opiates and cocaine, with a maximum jail sentence of 10 years and a fine of £1000 for possession or trafficking.

Several pop stars soon fell foul of this, and Mick Jagger and Keith Richards of the Rolling Stones were famously arrested at Richards' house in February 1967, allegedly after a tip-off from the *News of the World*. The circumstances of their arrest have provided journalists and scandalmongers with a feast of lurid and far-fetched stories over the years, but the reality is that Richards was found guilty of allowing his house to be used for the smoking of marijuana while Jagger was found guilty of possessing speed (four tablets). The former received a prison sentence of one year and the latter a sentence of three months, eliciting a wonderful editorial from William Rees-Mogg of *The Times* entitled *Who breaks a butterfly on a wheel* in which he wrote:

There must remain a suspicion in this case that Mr Jagger received a more severe sentence than would have been thought proper for any purely anonymous young man.

Both performers were eventually freed on appeal, though Jagger only received a conditional discharge. They were the first of a string of famous offenders charged with possession of marijuana, including Paul McCartney, John Lennon and Bob Marley.

Certainly the pop music industry of the 60s, and probably the film industry too, seems to have been borne along on a wave of marijuana. Richard Lester, director of the Beatles' film *Help*, is reputed to have claimed that the aroma of cannabis smoke pervaded the set at all times. The many on-screen antics of the stars would certainly support this assertion.

These arrests triggered widespread demand for law reform and famously led to a newspaper advertisement placed in *The Times* by the group SOMA (Society of Mental Awareness). Sixty-five liberals and freethinkers, including Francis Crick (of DNA fame), the critic Kenneth Tynan, Graham Greene and the photographer David Bailey signed a statement that declared 'the law against cannabis is immoral in principle and unworkable in practice'.

The newspaper comment accompanying these famous arrests and this advertisement caused the UK Government to review the dangers of marijuana, and Baroness Wootton, a well respected sociologist, was commissioned to investigate these matters. In the event her report of January 1969 made uncomfortable reading for a government intent on establishing the dangers of cannabis use. Interestingly the report cited not only the La Guardia Report but the original Indian Hemp Drugs Commission of 1894. This had heard evidence from more than 1000 witnesses on the use of hemp by all sections of the Indian community. Typical was the statement made by Colonel Alexander Crombie, one-time surgeon superintendent at Calcutta Hospital, who claimed 'My servant who uses ganja or bhang in excess is always at his post and capable of doing his duty'.

The Commission's chairman, Sir William Mackworth Young, had concluded 'On the whole the weight of evidence is to the effect that moderation in the use of the hemp drugs is not injurious to health'.

Having considered all of the evidence, Baroness Wootton concluded: 'Long-term consumption of cannabis in moderate doses has no harmful effects... and is very much less dangerous than the opiates, amphetamines, and barbiturates, and also less dangerous than alcohol'.

She also made two recommendations for some easing of the restrictions for cannabis:

Possessions of a small amount of cannabis should not normally be regarded as a serious crime to be punished by imprisonment... Preparations of cannabis and its derivatives should continue to be available on prescription for purposes of medical treatment.

The Government promptly ignored these liberalising aspects of her report and passed the Misuse of Drugs Act in 1971, which divided drugs into three classes of increasing danger. Class A included morphine, heroin, LSD and cocaine and class B included amphetamines, cannabis products and barbiturates, while class C was a miscellany of medical products that were in principle abusable.

Interestingly, at about the same time (1970), the US Government introduced the Comprehensive Drug Abuse Prevention and Control Act, which downgraded possession of cannabis products to a misdemeanour. The Canadian Government followed suit in 1972. President Jimmy Carter was probably the most liberal in his views on marijuana, and in an address to Congress in August 1978 he warned against severe penalties for possession of a drug that were more harmful than the drug itself. 'Nowhere is this more clear than in the law against possession of marijuana in private for personal use' he told Congress.

However, at the present time, importation of the drug into the USA can still attract a life sentence or even the death penalty in some states. Similar severe penalties still exist in Malaysia and Singapore.

Since then there have been a number of attempts to decriminalise the drug in the UK. The Runciman Report of 2000 suggested that cannabis products should be reclassified to class C, and while David Blunkett was Home Secretary this reclassification did occur (in 2002), with the police gradually taking a more tolerant attitude to the possession of small quantities of cannabis for personal and private use. In particular, the growing awareness that the medicinal properties of cannabis were more substantial than had been realised encouraged this more enlightened view. However, this was not to last for very long, due to the rise in the number of 'cannabis farms' growing the resin-rich form of cannabis known as *skunk*. These 'farms' range in size from domestic garages to full-size nurseries with full hydroponic facilities. The Government's response has been to introduce legislation that included a reclassification of cannabis to category B from 2009.

The medicinal properties of cannabis have been known for millennia. As well as the documented use by the great Persian physician Rhazes, the famous English herbalist Culpeper in his *Complete Herbal* (1653) sings the praises of hemp for allaying 'troublesome humours of the bowels and inflammation of the head, and other parts', and also claims its value in the treatment of gout, jaundice and worms. But it was in Victorian times that preparations like Squire's Extract and Dr J Collis Browne's Chlorodyne (already mentioned under 'Opium') became popular for the treatment of everything from incontinence, neuralgia and infantile convulsions to anthrax, cholera and rabies.

Both these proprietary preparations contained extracts of hashish in alcohol, though Chlorodyne contained quantities of morphine and chloroform as well. The Edinburgh-educated Irish physician Dr William O'Shaughnessy observed the use of Indian hemp while working in India, and popularized the use of tincture of cannabis resin in London on his return. He advocated it especially as an anti-convulsive remedy, though he did note that injudicious use could lead to a *strange balancing gait and perpetual giggling.* Various other Victorian physicians noted its value in the treatment of chronic headache, for example C R Marshall in 1905 claimed 'It appears to be useful in headache of a dull, continuous character'.

A brief foray into the isolation of cannabinoids took place in 1896, but it was not until 1940 that Alexander Todd and his group at Cambridge and Roger Adams at the University of Illinois isolated and provided a structure for cannabinol, an inactive constituent of the plant. It took a further 23 years before Mechoulam and Shivo at the Weissman Institute in Israel provided a structure for cannabidiol - also inactive - and finally the major psychoactive constituent $\triangle$9 - tetrahydrocannabinol succumbed to the structural investigations of Mechoulam and Gaoni, also at the Weissman Institute, in 1964.

Altogether nearly 500 discrete compounds have been isolated from *Cannabis sativa*, but only $\triangle$9-THC has any appreciable psychoactive activity. Mechoulam and Gaoni were also responsible for the first chemical synthesis of $\triangle$9-THC in 1967, and since then a whole range of natural cannabinoids and analogues have been prepared. Most have proved to be inactive in psychoactivity studies.

One novel chemical compound that has begun to achieve some notoriety first appeared in the laboratory of John W Huffman of Clemson University in 1995, when he prepared what he termed JWH-018. When he tested this compound he found it to be four to five times more potent than THC, despite having a very different chemical structure. It was also much easier to prepare than THC and soon attracted the attentions of 'amateur'chemists who made Huffman's compound for sale as a new designer drug or 'legal high'. Their various preparations have been sold on the internet under the names Spice Gold and Spice Yucatan Fire. For a while they became very popular, but they have now been banned in many countries. The chemical synthesis of legal highs has become a large industry over the past decade and the scale of operations ranges from domestic garages to sophisticated laboratories in Eastern Europe and China.

As with opium and its products, the obvious question every investigator wanted to know was - why does this unusual structure have psychoactive properties? A partial answer came in 1988 with the discovery of mammalian cannabinoid receptors, that is proteins within the body that interact with $\triangle$9-THC and trigger off a response. In the event, two types of receptors were identified, so called CB1 and CB2, with the former most prevalent in the brain and to a lesser extent in the lungs, liver and kidneys, while the latter is mainly confined to peripheral cells of the immune system and the spleen. Once activated, there is a triggering of changes in various neurotransmitter levels, and this probably explains the euphoriant activities and also the changes in cognition and memory.

Interestingly, activation of CB1 receptors in the liver increases fat production and at least one of the new anti-obesity drugs – ribonabant (Acomplia) – acts by inhibiting CB1 receptor activation.

Of course this was only part of the answer, since it still raised the question of why mammals have receptors that interact with a chemical compound from *Cannabis sativa*. The answer came in 1992, again from Mechoulam's research group, with the isolation of a fatty acid derivative - arachidonylethanolamide - which also bound to cannabinoid receptors and elicited similar effects to those produced by $\triangle$9-THC. They christened this anandamide, from the Sanskrit ananda meaning bliss or delight, and it proved to be the first of eight endogenous cannabinoids. These substances appear to be involved in pain control, in regulation of feeding behaviour, in control of the pleasure response, in memory, and a whole host of other neural responses.

For a while in the late 1990s it seemed they might also be responsible for the all-too-guilty pleasures associated with chocolate consumption. A paper in *Nature* in 1996 claimed that anadamide was present in chocolate at very low levels, but later studies failed to confirm the presence of anandamide in chocolate, so the neurological basis of chocolate's appeal still remains elusive.

Given the presence of cannabinoid receptors in the body, cannabis use has been investigated for a number of medical conditions over the past ten years or so. Its anti-emetic effect has been known since the days of the hippies in the early 1970s, and both $\triangle$9-THC and a synthetic analogue called nabilone have been used in conjunction with cancer chemotherapy. In fact the synthetic analogue nabilone is more effective than many other anti-emetic agents and also appears to enhance the appetites of cancer patients and AIDS patients. $\triangle$9-THC has also been shown to restrict the growth of certain types of brain tumour cells and prostate cancer cells, but we do not yet know how this works.

In addition, the use of cannabis in conjunction with more conventional drugs has been shown to alleviate some of the symptoms of multiple sclerosis and arthritis, and the British Medical Association recommended legalisation of cannabis for these purposes in 1997. Courts in the UK and USA have proved unsympathetic and have thus far rejected this proposal, while the governments of the Netherlands, New South Wales and Canada have relaxed the rules governing the cultivation of cannabis for personal medical use.

The situation has improved significantly in the last couple of years with the launch of a drug called Sativex by the UK company GW Pharmaceuticals. This is a mixture of $\triangle$9-THC and tetrahydrocannabinol, and appears to have considerable value for alleviation of the symptoms of MS and also for the relief of cancer pain. Sativex has been licensed for use in the UK, Canada, Spain and Germany, and may soon be available in Japan and Australia.

Of course the trick would be to produce an analogue of THC that binds to cannabinoid receptors and produces analgetic and other useful effects without inducing euphoria etc, but this has not yet been accomplished. For those who suffer from various kinds of neuropathic pain which is not easily treated with regular analgesics, the kind of experience described by Baudelaire in *Les Paradis Artificiels* would probably be welcome:

Time had completely disappeared. In a minute it was night, then it was daytime. The whole night was little more than a second.

WITCHCRAFT AND ORGIES

Belladonna, mandrake and daturas

The witches confess, that on certain days or nights they anoint a staff and ride on it to the appointed place.

This report from the trial of an alleged witch in 1470 is pretty much in line with most of the documentation from European sources for the 15th to 17th centuries. A Belgian 'witch', Claire Goessen, confessed in 1603 that 'she allowed herself to be transported by means of a stick anointed with unguent'.

But who were the witches, and what was the nature of the unguent or witches' salve? There are two contrasting possible answers to the first question. You may wish to suspend disbelief and soak up the occultism presented by Montague Summers in his well-known book *History of Witchcraft and Demonology* (1928). Alternatively, you can consider the much less extreme views of the well-respected Egyptologist Margaret Murray in her book *The Witch-cult in Western Europe* (first published by Oxford University Press in 1921). She proposed that witchcraft was a pre-Christian cult that revered Nature in all its forms with a special emphasis on fertility, and with a pagan deity who was probably bisexual.

Although Ms Murray's views attracted considerable controversy, it is certainly true that European magic and sorcery had their roots in Graeco-Roman pagan cults, and these were later complemented by Viking, Norse and Celtic folk practices. All of these incorporated the Roman goddess Diana (or an equivalent deity), who had a strong association with what was called the Wild Hunt. This was depicted as a wild orgiastic night-time hunt involving animals, wraiths and spirits.

The great pagan festivals of Walpurgis (the evening of April 30th), Midsummer's Eve (June 20th , the eve of the summer solstice) and All Hallows Eve (October 31st, the last day of the pagan year) also involved wild orgiastic celebrations and bonfires. Together these pagan rituals provided the basis for the witches' Sabbat where the witches were said to dance around a man dressed in black (*le diable*) or a large black cat (*un grand chat noir*), and wild sexual activities were claimed to occur.

So who were the women who became involved in these weird activities? First of all it is important to note that in the 15th to 17th centuries women did most of the food preparation and cooking, and were also healers and midwives. In consequence any problems with food or beer becoming tainted, or women dying in childbirth, or folk medicines killing the patients – in fact any kind of bad luck - could be laid at their door. Midwives, in particular, came under increasing suspicion during this period, and it was often claimed that these women would offer newborn babies to the devil during special post-delivery baptisms.

From around 1450 a witch craze gripped Europe which lasted for almost 200 years, exacerbated by the great conflict between the Protestant and Catholic religions, and women became the major target for this paranoia. The infamous publication *Malleus*

Maleficarum (*Hammer of the Witches*), written by the Dominican friars Heinrich Kramer and Jacob Sprenger, who were also participants in the Inquisition, was published in 1486. This encouraged a belief in magic and witchcraft of all kinds and although banned by the Catholic Church, it served as a manual for witch-hunting throughout the 16th and 17th centuries. Amongst other things it claimed that witches were usually women, since women were more stupid, weaker and more carnal than men, and that they changed their shapes, flew through the air and concocted magic ointments. Similar claims were made in *De Secretus Mulierum* (*Women's Secrets*):

Women are so full of venom in their time of menstruation that they poison animals by their glance, they infect children in the cradle; and whenever men have sexual intercourse with them, they are made leprous and sometimes cancerous.

Given this climate of fear and suspicion, it is hardly surprising that throughout Europe thousands of women were arrested and confessions were wrung from them through use of the thumbscrew, water torture, strappado and the rack. The British Isles were spared the very worst excesses of the Inquisition and witch trials were relatively few in number.

One of the most famous trials followed accusations against Alice Kyteler in 1324, an alleged witch from Kilkenny. It represents one of the first documented cases where an ointment was mentioned:

In rifleing the closet of the ladie, they found a pipe of ointment, wherewith she greased a staffe, upon which she ambled and galloped through thick and thin.

The full list of charges included associations with demons, the practice of various sorceries, the making of potions in the skull of a decapitated felon and using sorcery to kill or enfeeble each of her four husbands. In the event she was never brought to trial, since she escaped to England leaving several of her associates to face her accusers. One of these, Petronella of Meath, confessed under torture to sorcery and was burned at the stake.

There is overwhelming support for the belief that witches rubbed their bodies with an ointment or salve which led to levitation using animals, broomsticks, stools, or pitchforks. Gianbattista della Porta, a friend of Galileo, described how the witches rubbed ointment on their bodies:

They anoint the parts of the body, having rubbed them very thoroughly before, so that they grow rosy... and they think they are carried off to banquets, music, dances, and coupling with young men.

A similar story was told (in 1584) by Reginald Scot, who identified some of the ingredients of the ointment:

Blood of a flitter mouse, solanum somniferum, and oleum... they rubbe all parts of their bodys exceedinglie, till they looke red, and be verie hot, so as the pores may be opened, and their flesh soluble and loose... by this means in a moonlit night they seeme to be carried in the aire.

From a very long catalogue of alleged constituents, including soot and aconite (unlikely, due to its great toxicity), the three famous hexing herbs emerge from most recipes. These were deadly nightshade (*Atropa belladonna*), black henbane (*Hyoscyamus niger*) and mandrake (*Mandragora officinarum*). All of these contain chemical substances called tropane alkaloids, most importantly atropine and hyoscine (scopolamine), with the latter as the most probable facilitator of (apparent) levitation. Scopolamine is a powerful elicitor of hallucinations, especially involving shape and vision, and leads ultimately to narcosis, while atropine will cause disorientation and hallucinations, leading in toxic doses to respiratory failure, paralysis and death.

If you were a witch, the trick was to get the scopolamine into the brain without exceeding the toxic dose. The alkaloid is absorbed rapidly from the gastrointestinal tract but it is also easily absorbed through mucosal surfaces – the armpits and genital region – and here the anointed broomstick would have played a key role. In addition, the use of fat in the ointment and the rubbing of the skin until it was red would have ensured uptake through the skin. Once in the bloodstream, scopolamine penetrates the blood brain barrier very effectively (unlike atropine) and then causes depression of the central nervous system. An initial feeling of drowsiness and amnesia would have been followed by euphoria, hallucinations and finally narcosis. These responses will be familiar to anyone who received premedication before surgery back in the days when the NHS took a more relaxed view of surgical procedures and was less concerned about the turnaround of patients. These premedications typically contained scopolamine and opiates, and receiving them is the closest most people will have come to experiencing the effects of a witch's salve.

Of the other hexing herbs, the mandrake root has the most interesting folk history, and various preparations have been used for at least five thousand years. Some of the mystique surrounding the plant undoubtedly arises from the appearance of the root. This is often shaped like the letter Y, and thus may be compared with the human form, so opening the opportunity for use in magic, though it was also valued as an adjunct to surgery and as a poison.

Not surprisingly, the magicians, herbalists and apothecaries dreamed up ever more imaginative means of ensuring that this valuable commodity did not fall into the wrong hands. The Greek herbalist Theophrastus (third century BC) was among the first to describe a collection procedure involving a circle cut around the plant with a sword prior to uprooting while facing towards the west. Pliny the Elder (first century AD) also wrote of the foul stench produced during the uprooting. The Jewish historian Josephus (first century AD) provided more details, including the use of a dog tied to the root to assist with the uprooting. Most later descriptions, including a large number of murals and woodcuts, also mention or depict a dog tied to the root, but add something about the dreadful shriek emanating from the root at the moment of removal from the soil. This awful sound was alleged to kill the dog and render mad anyone who heard it. Hence:

> Then on the still night air,
> The bark of a dog is heard,
> A shriek! A groan!
> A human cry. A trumpet sound,
> The mandrake root lies captive on the ground.

While the author of that particular verse is not known, the references in Shakespeare to the same events are well documented as when Juliet says (in *Romeo and Juliet*):

> Shrieks like mandrakes, torn out of the ground,
> That living mortals, hearing them, run mad.

J K Rowling has now brought this myth to a wider audience through Harry Potter. It was depicted graphically in the second film, *Harry Potter and the Chamber of Secrets*, where the pupils in the practical class being taught by Professor Sprout had to put on ear protectors before uprooting their screeching mandrakes.

The beneficial medical uses of mandrake were described by William Turner in his *New Herball*, which appeared in three parts between 1551 and 1568. He suggested that:

If mandragora be taken out of measure by and by slepe ensueth and a great lousing of the strygthe with a forgetfulness.

Shakespeare confirmed the soporific effect of mandrake in *Antony and Cleopatra* (Act 1, Scene 5):

Give me to drink mandragora,
That I might sleep out this great gap of time
My Anthony is away.

Renaissance poisoners like Lucrezia Borgia are alleged to have fermented the root until it stank, then stored it for a further 60 days until a greenish pulp was obtained. This was administered to the victim, who then suffered trembling, stomach pains and yellowing of the eyes before they died. If the victim suspected that this was something a bit worse than a dose of dysentery or the effects of too much alcohol, there was apparently an antidote. Unfortunately it called for honey, butter, oatmeal, mint leaves, anise, nutmeg, fennel seed, clove bark, ginger, cinnamon, celery, radish and dill, and while these ingredients might be found in the modern kitchens of those addicted to the television chefs, they would have been rather less common in the average Renaissance kitchen. The victim would have to seek help from the local apothecary, who might well have made up the poison in the first place!

The 20th century poisoner Dr Crippen was able to obtain his hyoscine (scopolamine) from a pharmacy in New Oxford Street. He used this to poison his wife Cora, though he also shot her for good measure. He subsequently cut her up and either burned the body parts or dissolved them in acid, but he was careless enough to leave a few parts in the basement of his house. He was eventually apprehended and convicted because traces of scopolamine were detected in fragments of Cora's stomach, kidneys, liver, and intestines.

All these activities took place in Europe or the Middle East using the classical hexing herbs, but in the Americas *Brugmansia* plants containing the tropane alkaloids, especially scopolamine, were also used for magic and divination. All these have large, bell-shaped flowers, and seeds from them were ground to a powder and made into a beverage which was much prized for its divinatory properties. The following is a report from an unnamed traveller in Peru in 1846:

The native fell into a heavy stupor, his eyes vacantly fixed on the ground, his mouth convulsively closed, and his nostrils dilated. In the course of a quarter of an hour, his eyes began to roll, foam issued from his mouth, and his whole body was agitated by frightful convulsions.

Many related plant species which are widely distributed around the world also contain varying amounts of atropine and scopolamine. One of these is still used in Asia (often mixed with cannabis and tobacco) for fevers, skin diseases and analgesia, while others are used by various Indian tribes in South America for divination and for infanticide -- breastfeeding mothers were known to smear their breasts with plant extract to kill unwanted babies. Most infamous of all was *Datura stramonium*, known as devil's trumpet, thornapple and jimson weed, which was primarily used for seduction and induction of temporary madness. The name derives from Jamestown and probably relates to an occasion when British soldiers were drugged by the settlers in Virginia to prevent them apprehending some local renegades (in 1676). Several descriptions of the effects of this scopolamine intoxication were recorded at the time:

Some of them having eaten plentifully became fools for several days, one would blow up a feather in the air, another sit naked like a monkey, or fondly kiss and paw his companions, and sneer in their faces.

To this day extracts of *D. stramonium* are used by thieves in South American cities to drug their victims so that on awakening they have no recollection of what has befallen them. On a more positive note, cigarettes made from the plant, cannabis and lobelia have been used to treat asthma, and some benefit may be obtained due to the relaxation of bronchial muscles it produces.

The most instructive and most quoted modern description of *Datura*-induced intoxication and hallucination was provided by the Mexican Carlos Castaneda, who experimented with 'flying ointment' given to him by Yaqui Indians of Northern Mexico in 1968. He reported:

The motion of my body was slow and shaky... The momentum carried me forward one more step, which was even more elastic and longer than the preceding one. And from there I soared... I saw the dark sky above me, and the clouds going by me... I enjoyed such freedom and swiftness as I had never known before.

In recent years many of Castaneda's reports of his experiences have been called into question as works of fiction.

On the other side of the world in Australia, plants of the family *Duboisia* are also a rich source of scopolamine. The species *Duboisia hopwoodii* has always been especially prized by the Aborigines and extracts (known as *pituri*) are used primarily to alleviate fatigue. In the past the Aborigines chewed the plant much as the South Americans Indians chewed coca, but now they smoke it in admixture with tobacco. Joseph King who was one of the few survivors of the

121

ill-fated Burke and Wills expedition that attempted to cross the central deserts of Australia, recalled how he was found by Aborigines and given *pituri* to help him revive.

The final hexing herb was henbane, which as far back as the time of Pliny the Elder was being recommended for its sedative effect:

It is certainly known, that if one take of it in drink more than four leaves, it will put him beside himself.

A more recent account of the effects of inhaling the smoke from smouldering seeds of henbane was given by Gustave Schenk in 1966:

Each part of my body seemed to be going off on its own, and I was seized with the fear that I was falling apart. At the same time, I experienced an intoxicating sensation of flying.

We will never know exactly what happened at the Witches' Sabbats and how much of what they related of their activities had been wrung from them under torture, but the effects of the tropane alkaloids were eloquently described by Louis Lewin at the end of the nineteenth century. In his *Phantastica* he states:

The disagreeable symptoms of these Solanaceae and their active elements, atropine and scopolamine that give rise to hallucinations and illusions of sight, hearing and taste.

And he was in no doubt about the malevolent effects of these compounds:

These substances in suitable doses may give rise to a state of dementia lasting for hours and even days. I am certain that it has frequently been employed for purely criminal purposes... and have served to intoxicate girls and seduce them to immoral acts.

If only the witches had known a bit more about the dangerous properties of the drugs they were taking, they might well have thought twice before using them, or at least been able to mount a credible defence at their trials!

CHAPTER EIGHT

HEARTS AND MINDS

Peyote, mescaline and amphetamines

There is another herb......of the earth. It is called peiotl. It is white. It is found in the North Country. Those who eat or drink it see visions, either frightful or laughable (visions espantosas o irrisibles).

Once again the Franciscan missionary Bernadino de Sahagun gives us the first and most precise description of a South American hallucinogenic preparation, in this instance the one from the peyote cactus *Lophophora williamsii*. This entry comes from his *Historia General de las Cosas de Nueva Espana* first published in 1557, which also includes descriptions of *ololiuqui* and other magical preparations.

The grey-green, spineless cactus is commonly found in Central Mexico and parts of the South Western USA, and there is evidence from meso-American caves in Texas that early American cultures may have used this cactus more than 5000 years ago. There are certainly reports by Francisco Hernandez, who travelled with Cortes, of its use by the Aztecs as a divinatory plant. In the 1950s, the ethnobotanist Richard Evans Schultes met several shamans who described to him the importance of the cactus for the Huichol people of central Mexico. They still have an annual ceremonial hunt for the cactus during the autumn, followed by a kind of harvest festival in January when the peyote is consumed. Schultes also noted how after consumption of the peyote, the intoxicated participants spent several days dancing and chanting, and offering prayers to their Gods.

All of these cultures used the crown of the cactus to produce slices, now called mescal buttons, and four to thirty of these were consumed as part of pseudo religious celebrations. From about 1690, the Amerindians of Mexico elevated these celebrations to a form of mass or eucharist where mescal buttons were consumed in place of the 'host', activities that did not endear them to the Catholic Church.

The American Indians from further north, primarily Mescaleros Apaches, Comanches and Kiowas, appear to have discovered the use of peyote while on raiding missions, and brought the custom back to their tribal lands. Here a new religious cult developed from about 1880 which became known as the Native American Church. It grew in popularity until it numbered more than 13000 worshippers by the 1920s. Today the number of active adherents is in excess of one million, many of whom are Navajo Indians.

Various attempts were made over the years by the US Government to eradicate this cult, with claims that consumption of peyote led to licentious and drunken behaviour. During several well publicised court battles, the Indians were able to prove that in contrast to popular opinion, peyote use encouraged abstemious behaviour and allowed communication with God rather than anti-social behaviour. Finally in 1967, the US Congress voted to allow the use of peyote by adherents of the Native American Church. This was followed by the Religious Freedom Restoration Act of 1993, which resulted from a Supreme Court ruling in 1990 in favour of two Native American Indians who had been fired from their jobs after testing positive for mescaline. They claimed they had used peyote as part of religious devotions. These days it is possible to obtain mescal buttons by secure mail order using the US Postal Service.

Over the years a number of well known authors have written about their experiences with peyote, and most agree that after initial ingestion there are unpleasant effects including nausea and vomiting, and perhaps anxiety attacks, but this is followed by coloured visions, heightened perception of sound and smell, and a sense of well-being. The effective dose is around a quarter to a half gram of mescaline and the psychoactive experience may last for up to 12 hours.

One of the first to describe the effects in detail was Louis Lewin in his all encompassing book *Phantastica: Narcotic and Stimulating Drugs*. In this he talks about his first experiments with peyote which commenced in 1888:

Coloured arabesques and figures appear in endless play… geometrical forms of all kinds, spheres and cubes rapidly changing colour, triangles with yellow dots from which emanate golden and silver strings, radiant tapestries, carpets, filigree lacework in blue, brilliant red, green, blue and yellow stripes… trees with light-yellow blossoms, and many things besides.

He quite reasonably suggests that in the Indian mind this would be an evocation or personification of God.

Probably the most famous user was Aldous Huxley who described his experiences in the book *The Doors of Perception*, published in 1954. His main contention was that survival of an individual required what he called the 'mind at large' to be funnelled through 'the reducing valve of the brain and nervous system' and that mescaline removed these constraints. However, he believed that this occurred as a result of a diminished supply of glucose to the brain rather than (as we now know) due to changes in the levels of neurotransmitters. So an experience with mescaline allowed the consumer to be 'shaken out of the ruts of ordinary perception, to be shown for a few timeless hours, the outer and the inner world… as they are apprehended… by the Mind at Large'.

In May 1953, having consumed 0.4 g of mescaline, Huxley reported the usual array of visual illusions, such that a flower arrangement became 'what Adam had seen on the morning of his creation – the miracle, moment by moment, of naked existence'. A self-portrait of the artist Cézanne in a book that he had in front of him came to life 'as a small goblin-like man looking out through a window in the page before me'.

These initial experiences must have been especially exciting for Huxley, since he had suffered from seriously impaired vision following a staphylococcal infection when he was seventeen. Huxley went on to write a second book entitled *Heaven and Hell* in which he further examined the benefits and importance of visionary experiences and concluded that the mescaline experience:

Throws light on the hitherto unknown regions of his (the consumer's) own mind; and at the same time it throws light, indirectly, on other minds, more richly gifted in respect of vision than his own... he comes to a new and better understanding of the ways those other minds perceive and feel and think.

On the day that he died, November 22nd 1963, Huxley used LSD to help him achieve a gentle passing, so he was certainly unaware that earlier that day President John F. Kennedy had been assassinated in Dallas. Huxley is, of course, remembered most for his many novels, including most notably *Brave New World*, but *The Doors of Perception* remains one of the most significant practical and philosophical treatises on the use of drugs for aiding introspection. It is also famous, so it is alleged, as the inspiration for the name used by the rock band the Doors. Also like Timothy Leary and Aleister Crowley, Huxley appears on the sleeve of the Beatles' Sergeant Pepper album.

Rather similar experiences were reported by Havelock Ellis, a British physician and social commentator who was probably the first to write openly about homosexuality and many other aspects of sexual relations in his hugely influential series entitled *Studies in the Psychology of Sex*. His own marriage was unusual since his wife Edith was a lesbian and he himself was allegedly impotent, though he could apparently be aroused by the sight of a woman urinating. His many books and essays on the subject of sex were complemented by several books of poems and a translation of Zola's *Germinal*. It is perhaps not surprising that such a polymath would experiment with drugs and he wrote of his experiences (in the *Contemporary Review*) after consuming three mescal button on Good Friday 1897:

In the course of the evening, they (images) became distinct... mostly a vast field of golden jewels, studded with red and green stones, ever changing... they would spring into flower-like forms and then turn into gorgeous butterfly forms or endless folds of glistening, iridescent, fibrous wings of wonderful insects.

Perhaps of more interest was his comparison of the effects of the various drugs he had tried:

Under the influence of alcohol, the intellect is impaired; haschisch again produces an uncontrollable tendency to movement and bathes its victim in a sea of emotion. The mescal drinker remains calm and collected amid the sensory turmoil around him... it may be claimed that the artificial paradise of mescal is safe and dignified beyond its peers.

These very personal literary excursions using the natural product mescaline have to be compared with the very public and large-scale use and abuse of the amphetamines, which are chemically synthesised structural analogues of mescaline. The story begins with the investigations in the early 1920s on the Chinese herbal medicine known as *Ma huang* from the plants *Ephedra sinaica* and *Ephedra vulgaris*. These extracts had been in continuous use since about 3000 BC for the relief of coughing and fever. In the 19th century the extracts were known colloquially as 'teamster's tea' and 'whorehouse tea', to identify their alleged activities as stimulants for truck drivers and brothel patrons respectively.

When ephedrine was isolated from these plants and tested on dogs, it produced similar effects to those elicited by adrenaline - increased blood pressure and accelerated heart rate. Further studies in the USA revealed that ephedrine produced a sustained bronchodilator effect in the lungs, and this had great potential for the treatment of asthma. It was approved for this purpose by the American Medical Association in 1926. It was soon being synthesised, and one analogue, Benzedrine, was shown to be an excellent nasal decongestant; it was sold in the form of an inhaler from 1932.

Benzedrine was also called amphetamine, and had first been synthesised in 1887 by Lazar Edeleanu at the University of Berlin. It quickly became apparent that it was a powerful stimulant in the central nervous system as well as a decongestant, and during World War II, Benzedrine and the more potent methylamphetamine (Methedrine, 'speed'), first synthesised in 1929, and dexamphetamine (Dexedrine), were used by the armed forces to alleviate fatigue. They were also much employed in the Korean and Vietnam Wars.

After WWII amphetamines became widely available as prescription drugs for the treatment of obesity, post-natal depression and for stress, and in some countries, like Japan, they were considered safe enough to be purchased over the counter. This combination of ready availability and the emerging drugs culture of the 1960s almost inevitably led to amphetamines becoming yet another agent of abuse. Intravenous use of methedrine was a particularly prevalent and dangerous practice, hence the slogan 'speed kills'.

In the spring of 1969, the body formed between the Haight Ashbury Free Medical Clinic and the Student Association for the Study of Hallucinogens (STASH), published a review of the situation regarding amphetamines and related drugs in its house magazine, *Journal of Psychedelic Drugs*. In this they described a typical 'speed freak' as someone who had tried oral amphetamines before progressing to limited experimentation with cannabis and heroin and finally to intravenous use of amphetamines. The first experience was almost universally described euphorically, eg 'my whole body was just doing a physiological flip-flop'. This initial ecstatic experience led inexorably to the use of many daily injections of perhaps 200mg each time, with resultant insomnia that would last for several days before a 'crash' and several days of uninterrupted sleep. On waking the whole process would be repeated.

Inevitably a high degree of anorexia developed and viral hepatitis from dirty needles was not uncommon – later HIV would be a more serious complication. Other complications included a crawling sensation under the skin – 'you start to feel like there's bugs going around under your skin and you know they're not there, but you pick at them anyway'. An increasing level of paranoia was also common and suicidal tendencies often developed.

The popularity of amphetamines in the San Francisco Bay area supported at this time as many as six to eight large-volume 'speed laboratories', providing perhaps 75% of the local demand, while numerous 'bathroom' operations provided the rest of the supply. These household laboratories used simple equipment available from hardware stores, with household appliances like hairdryers to drive off the water from the initially wet products. The basic chemistry was very simple, and since the various chemicals were undoubtedly sourced from industrial or university chemistry laboratories, the 'bathroom chemists' were mainly real chemists with experience of the necessary procedures.

Interestingly, the slightly impure amphetamines that evolved from these operations were more highly prized than the purer versions. This impure product, known as 'flash speed', apparently produced a 'heavy flash' when used intravenously, characterised by a rapid and almost orgiastic pleasurable response. The purer form of the drug produced its response more slowly, though the experience was longer lasting. As with all other drugs, the initially produced drugs were often mixed or 'cut' with other inactive ingredients, eg talcum powder, baking soda, monosodium glutamate etc, and much of the violence associated with amphetamine use centred around those dealers who were caught dealing in inferior products.

The drugs also began to appear in sport; amphetamines are particularly favoured by cyclists, who value the sudden and explosive boost they provide. Sportsmen christened them *la bombe and la bomba*. A combination of dexamphetamine and the barbiturate amylobarbitone called Drinamyl became the mainstay of the club scene, and since this was prescribed in the form of a blue, lozenge-shaped pill, they became known as 'purple hearts'. The sporadic battles that flared up in Britain between the scooter-riding 'mods' and the motor-bike riding 'rockers' in the 1960s, graphically depicted in the cult film *Quadrophenia*, were also claimed to have been fuelled by amphetamines. However, these beachfront spectacles were mostly due to the natural aggression of testosterone-laden males free from the strictures of national conscription and with nothing to do on Bank Holidays as they were to the use of drugs. In any case, most of the available drugs led to euphoria or somnolence rather than violent behaviour.

None the less, by the end of the 1960s amphetamine abuse was a more serious problem in the UK than use of cocaine, heroin or cannabis. Most of the amphetamines are classified in category B of the dangerous drugs list, while methamphetamine is in class A (with heroin and cocaine).

The scene was set for two drugs that more closely resembled mescaline in structure and also in psychoactive potency. The first, MDA (3,4-methylenedioxyamphetamine) was introduced in the 1960s as an aid to psychotherapy, and the second and more infamous MDMA (3,4-methylendioxy methamphetamine, or ecstasy) first appeared on the club scene in the 1970s. This had been studied by the US chemist and pharmacologist Alexander Shulgin in the early 1960s, and he initially promoted its therapeutic benefits.

Shulgin, born in Berkeley, California in 1925, is another of those larger-than-life characters who are associated with the psychoactive drug scene. His career began conventionally with undergraduate study of chemistry, interrupted by service in the US navy during World War II, and obtained a PhD in Biochemistry from the University of California, Berkeley. After several years in the pharmaceutical industry, he set up his own laboratory to make and test substances related to mescaline. Initially his extensive studies were supported by the US Drug Enforcement Agency (DEA) and he supplied the agency with drugs to evaluate, and also briefed their field agents about the affects of the drugs. This strange alliance began to unravel when he wrote about his experiences with mescaline and his new 'drugs' in a treatise entitled PiHKAL – Phenethylamines I have Known and Loved: a Chemical Love Story. This was in part an autobiographical novel, but it also provided full details of how to make more than 200 amphetamine-like substances. His recipes were very detailed and since the entire contents of PiHKAL are now available on the internet, this sourcebook of psychoactive substances is frequently cited in court cases involving illicit drug production.

Shulgin also gave a comprehensive description of his experiences after taking most of his substances. After 400 mg of mescaline he reported:

Everything seemed to have a humorous interpretation. People's faces are in caricature, small cars seem to be chasing big cars, and all cars coming towards me seem to have faces... The effect of the drug is the extreme empathy felt for all small things... One cannot pluck a flower, and even to walk upon a gravel path requires one to pick his footing carefully to avoid hurting or disturbing the stones.

Not surprisingly the US Drug Enforcement Authority investigated Shulgin's laboratory. Although they could not find any evidence of criminal activity, they none the less labelled *PiHKAL* as a 'cookbook for the synthesis of illegal drugs'.

Ecstasy became especially popular in clubs and was the mainstay of the 1980s rave culture, especially in the holiday resorts of Ibiza. It induces a feeling of euphoria and empathy (even love) for others, feelings which last for about 3-5 hours. The downside is the after-effects, which include fatigue, irritability and depression, and where the user has been involved in wild prolonged and vigorous dancing there can be serious dehydration and raised body temperature. There have been several well-publicised deaths where the ecstasy user had rehydrated to excess, leading to coma and death due to gross disruption of salt balance. However, these tragic deaths have to be seen in the context of the much larger number of deaths of young persons caused by drink-related traffic accidents.

A more dangerous drug first appeared in the Haight-Ashbury district in 1967 -DOM or 2,5-dimethoxy-4-methylamphetamine, which was one of Shulgin's 'magical half-dozen'. This produced effects akin to LSD, with wild coloured hallucinations and altered cognition, but the duration of action was about twice that of LSD, so there was more opportunity for self-harm. Mercifully this drug had a relatively short life since it was considered too dangerous for use by even hardened speed freaks.

Of much greater importance is a group of phenylethylamines christened the 2C* family and again popularised by Shulgin. His personal favourite was 2C-B or 4-bromo-2,5-dimethoxyphenylethylamine, whose effects (after taking 20mg) he described in ecstatic terms:

A sensation of lightness and rivulets of warmth began seeping through my body. Bright lights began pulsing and flashing behind my closed eyelids. My body was flooded with orgasms – practically from just breathing. The lovemaking was phenomenal, passionate, ecstatic, lyrical, animal, loving, tender, sublime. If there is anything ever found to be an effective aphrodisiac, it will probably be patterned after 2C-B.

It is hardly surprising that this drug has become popular. An increasing number of police raids on designer drug laboratories are discovering materials associated with 2C-B manufacture.

A new designer drug exploded onto the market and into the media from mid 2007. This was mephedrone or 4-methylmethcathinone, which although structurally related to methamphetamine it is more closely allied to the natural plant product cathinone from *Catha edulis*. This is the source of the euphoriant extract *khat* which has been used for many centuries by men in the Yemen and in Somalia. They chew khat from the late afternoon and become euphoriated and indolent. Over time many of them also become impotent, though the cause of this is unknown.

Since mephedrone was a member of a new class of substances it was not initially banned, although it possessed similar psychoactive properties to ecstasy. Unsurprisingly it quickly became popular as one of the new 'legal highs'. From 2007 mephedrone was widely available via the internet for as little as £10-15 per gram, with supplies originating mainly from China. By mid 2010 the drug had been detected across the whole of Europe and in North America, and a number of deaths had been linked (often tenuously) to its use. Many governments now moved to ban it.

In the UK, the increasing availability and use of mephedrone first caught the attention of the news media in the Autumn of 2009, and there was a spate of articles demonising what the press christened miao miao or meow meow. Headlines announced 'MP'S SON IS MEOW MEOW DRUG BARON', and emphasised that the drug was being used by up to 20% of secondary school attendees: 'SCHOOLS POWERLESS OVER KILLER DRUG'. This press excitement prompted the UK Government's Advisory Council on the Misuse of Drugs (ACMD) to send a report on mephedrone to the Home Secretary, Alan Johnson, suggesting that he arrange for pharmacological and toxicological evaluation to be carried out as a matter of urgency.

Johnson promptly announced on March 30th 2010 that the drug would be made illegal within days. This precipitated an unholy row with members of the ACMD, since they believed that any move to illegality prior to biological evaluation would serve only to criminalise the (mainly) young users of the drug.

This was not the first time the Home Secretary had ignored the advice of the ACMD, and it followed the precipitate sacking of the Council's previous chairman, David Nutt, on October 30th 2009. Nutt had spoken in a lecture at King's College London of his views that the use of ecstasy or cannabis was less dangerous than consumption of alcohol and tobacco. He went further and suggested that there were more deaths each year attributed to horse-riding accidents than to the use of ecstasy – a statistic that was actually correct. However these views were contrary to the Government view that ecstasy was a category A drug under the terms of the Misuse of Drugs Act (1971).

Several members of the ACMD resigned following Nutt's departure and others followed after this new disagreement over mephedrone. Johnson pressed on, and the Misuse of Drugs Act was eventually changed to allow new legal highs to be made temporarily illegal while their pharmacological activity was assessed. This was already the situation that existed in North America and Australasia, where new substances with analogous chemical structures to existing controlled substances could be banned while they were evaluated. The US Federal Analog Act, for example, covers all chemicals that are 'substantially similar' to known controlled substances.

All governments now face a burgeoning industry (especially in China) and increasingly sophisticated laboratories are producing dozens of new designer drugs each year, mostly modelled on the amphetamines. The chemistry is generally simple and the rewards are great.

Amidst all this controversy, one factor was largely overlooked - the growing concerns about contamination of ecstasy and cocaine in the UK. By mid 2010 most ecstasy tablets contained no MDMA at all and comprised mephedrone and fillers instead, so those purchasing drugs from dealers or via the internet had little idea of what they were actually consuming.

The well-known street drug angel dust or PCP was first introduced as the anaesthetic phencyclidine by Parke-Davis in 1995. The drug has only limited chemical similarity to the amphetamines, but it used to be very popular on the club scene. It is usually sprayed on to marijuana, mint or parsley leaves and this plant material is then smoked. When mixed with marijuana it is known as supergrass.

One final interesting amphetamine analogue is methylphenidate (Ritalin), which shares the usual stimulant effect on the CNS with the other amphetamines but appears to possess special efficacy in the parts of the cerebral cortex that are concerned with the control of attention. The drug is thus especially effective for children with attention-deficit hyperactivity disorder (ADHD). This condition is associated with hyperactive behaviour and an inability to concentrate, and can usually be successfully treated with two to three doses of 5-20mg of Ritalin per day.

The mode of action of all of these drugs appears to depend on their modulation of the functions of the neurotransmitters dopamine, serotonin and noradrenaline (norepinephrine). The potentiation of dopamine function is particularly relevant to the states of euphoria attained with mescaline and the amphetamines, since dopamine is intimately involved in triggering reward responses in various parts of the brain.

None of these drugs comes close to achieving what Aldous Huxley envisaged for his drug soma in *Brave New World* which allowed people to 'take a holiday from the reality of the daily lives'. In *The Doors of Perception* he summarised what was required:

A new drug which will relieve and console our suffering species without doing more harm in the long run than it does in the short. Such a drug must be potent in minute doses and synthesizable... It must be less toxic than opium and cocaine, less likely to produce undesirable social consequences than alcohol or barbiturates, less inimical to the heart and lungs than the tars and nicotine of cigarettes.

This wonder drug still awaits discovery, but in the meantime we can view a long history of intoxication ranging from the peiotl of the

Aztecs to the crystal meth of the Haight Ashbury and the ecstasy of the modern club scene. Somewhere along the line, the romance of communing with the gods has been lost. This 'romance' was eloquently described by one of the shamans who talked to Richard Evan Schultes:

Speak to the peyote with your hearts, with your thoughts, and the peyote sees your heart. And if you have luck, you will hear things and receive things that are invisible to others, but that God has given you to pursue your path.

DRUNK ON MUSHROOMS

Fly agaric

They are subject to various visions, terrifying or felicitous... owing to which some jump, some dance, others cry and suffer great terrors... But this applies only to those who overindulge, while those who use a small quantity experience a feeling of extraordinary lightness, joy, courage, and a sense of energetic well-being.

This translation of a report from the Russian Stephan Krasheninnikov, who travelled through Siberia in the early 1750s, was made by the ethnobotanist R Gordon Wasson, who worked with Albert Hofmann on the psychedelics of *Psilocybe* mushrooms. He included it in a book he wrote with his wife Valentina entitled Mushrooms, *Russia and History* (1957). The cause of the intoxication was the red and white spotted mushroom *Amanita muscaria* or fly agaric (named for its supposed insectidical properties), which held a fascination for Wasson for much of his life. He was a strong advocate of the theory that the 'divine soma' of ancient India was none other than fly agaric and his later book Soma: the *Divine Mushroom of Immortality* (1968) is devoted to this hypothesis.

Soma was the name for the divine drink taken by the deities described in the *Rig Vedas*, the 1000 or so sacred hymns written in Sanskrit around 800 BC which formed the basis for the Hindu religion. Despite a huge amount of scholarly work by Wasson and many other ethnobotanists and anthropologists, the identity of the plant from which Soma was obtained remains in doubt.

What is much better understood is the use of fly agaric by the tribes of Northern Russia, especially Siberia. Here we have well-substantiated reports from explorers and other visitors who all describe a beverage made from this mushroom. Probably the most cited report was that of the Swedish cartographer colonel Filip von Strahlenberg. He spent 12 years in captivity with the Koryak tribe, who were herders of reindeer in the Kamchatka peninsular of north-eastern Siberia. On his return in 1730, he related that the richer members of the tribe traded furs for quantities of fly agaric, which they valued highly, and which they used on feast days:

When they make a feast, they pour water upon some of the mushrooms, and boil them. Then they drink the liquor, which intoxicates them. The poorer sort… post themselves round the huts of the rich, and watch for the opportunity of the guests coming down to make water; and then hold a wooden bowl to receive the urine, which they drink off greedily, as having still some virtue of the mushroom in it, and by this way they also get drunk.

Several decades later, George Steller, a German botanist and zoologist who was the naturalist on a number of expeditions to the Kamchatka peninsula between 1734 and 1741, recorded in his journals a similar account of his experiences with the Koryak. These were published in 1774 some years after his death.
The fly agarics are dried, then eaten in large pieces without chewing them… After about half an hour the person becomes completely intoxicated and

140

experiences extraordinary visions. Those who cannot afford the high price (of the mushrooms) drink the urine of those who have eaten it, and become as intoxicated, if not more so. The urine seems to be more powerful than the mushroom, and its effect may last through the fourth or fifth man.

Louis Lewin in his *Phantastica* confirmed these observations:

As soon as the Koryak notices his inebriety decreasing, he drinks his own urine... this way the action may be renewed several times.

The pharmacology of this urine drinking is obviously fascinating, but it has not been properly investigated. For a long time it was believed that the main psychoactive constituent of fly agaric was a chemical substance called muscarine, which is active at one type of the receptors for the neurotransmitter acetylcholine. However, muscarine is only present in trace amounts in the mushroom. It was not until 1964-5 that researchers in England, Japan and Switzerland conclusively proved that the major biologically active constituents were in fact the substances ibotenic acid and muscimol, which is 5-10 times more potent. Muscimol rapidly crosses the blood-brain barrier and exerts its effects through interference with inhibitory neurotransmitters. While muscimol is rapidly metabolised, ibotenic is excreted unchanged in the urine within about 90 minutes. The hallucinogenic effects of urine drinking are thus probably due primarily to the effects of ibotenic acid being converted into muscimol.

Since there are still occasional instances of mushroom poisoning with fly agaric, the clinical features of consumption are well known and can be compared with the descriptions given above. Patients typically walk as if intoxicated with alcohol and in addition, exhibit muscle twitching and complain of hallucinations.

One of the problems with fly agaric is that patients and those using the mushroom for recreational purposes report widely differing effects.

Both the Wassons experimented with the mushroom in 1965 and 1966 and reported being disappointed with the results, especially in comparison with their experiences with *Psilocybe* mushrooms. At worst they felt nauseous and actually vomited, while at best they fell into a deep sleep with vivid dreams. Other experienced psychedelic drug users have also reported disappointing results, and the use of fly agaric has largely been abandoned, or only used when alternative 'tripping' materials are not available. And in a world gone mad with legislation about health and safety, the familiar red and white spotted mushroom has all but disappeared from children's books.

Fly agaric does not often occur in adult fiction, though H G Wells in his short story *The Purple Pileus* has the central character (Mr Coombes) undergo a massive character change after eating some of the eponymous mushroom. This dull and hen-pecked husband returns from a walk in the country during which he has attempted suicide using the mushroom. He then terrifies the guests at his wife's tea party, including trying to force-feed fly agaric to one of them, and then becomes the dominant partner in the marriage. Of more interest is the soma of Aldous Huxley's novel *Brave New World*, since this was a universal panacea and hallucinogen that alleviated the strains of everyday life. However, this was a synthetic drug, and there was never any suggestion that this was a naturally occurring substance.

In *Alice in Wonderland*, Alice eats or drinks a series of substances that make her grow or shrink. The famous caterpillar with the hookah persuades her to eat some of the mushroom on which he is seated, and after nibbling a portion she suffers another change of shape:

'Come, my head's free at last!' said Alice in a tone of delight, which changed into alarm in another moment, when she found that her shoulders were nowhere to be found; all she could see ,when she looked down, was an immense length of neck, which seemed to rise like a stalk out of a sea of green leaves that lay far below her.

Although both Lewis Carroll and his illustrator John Tenniel would have been familiar with Cooke's *Manual of British Fungi* and would have known of the hallucinogenic properties of fly agaric, there is no suggestion from Tenniel's illustration that either author or illustrator had fly agaric in mind.

One piece of nonsense that has been promulgated, often accompanied by serious anthropological arguments, is that the myth of Father Christmas, with his red and white coat, is somehow associated with the use of fly agaric. The only half-serious side to this suggestion is his use of flying reindeer, since in the wilds of Scandinavia these are known to occasionally consume fly agaric and thus become inebriated!

THE GREEN FAIRY

Absinthe

There are numerous references to the use of wormwood or *Artemisia absinthium* as a vermifuge (a substance for getting rid of parasitic worms), perhaps going back to biblical times, and certainly the Elizabethan herbalist Gerard cited its use for this purpose: 'wormewood voideth away the wormes of the guts'. The alcoholic brew of Tudor England called 'purl', which comprised a mixture of beer and wormwood, may also have had this activity. But here we are more concerned with the much stronger liquor whose effects Oscar Wilde summarised in his usual apposite fashion:

After the first glass you see things as you wish they were. After the second, you see things as they are not. Finally, you see things as they really are, and that is the most horrible thing in the world.

The origins of absinthe are obscure, but it is produced by distillation of a brandy strength liquor in which the plants *Artemisia absinthium*, anise (*Pimpinella anisum*), hyssop (*Hyssopus officinalis*), fennel (*Foeniculum vulgare*) and other herbs have been steeped. The invention of this strong, yellow liquor is usually attributed to two unmarried sisters called Henriod. They lived in the Swiss village of

Neuchâtel in the late 1760s and advertised their liquor as *bon extrait d'absinthe*. A little later (around 1792) a French doctor in the village of Couvet, Switzerland, by the name of Pierre Ordinaire also advertised an apparently similar liquor which he called *la fée verte* (green fairy). What is more certain is that Major Henri Dubied purchased the recipe for absinthe from the Henriod sisters in 1797. He, it is claimed, valued the *bon extrait* as a general cure-all and also as an aid to his sexual potency.

His daughter Emilie subsequently married Henri-Louis Pernod and the association of the names Pernod and absinthe would forever be linked. Father and son-in-law established a small distillery in Couvet, followed in 1805 by a much larger operation across the border in France, on the banks of the River Doubs in Pontarlier, which initially had an output of 400 litres of absinthe per day. With these two operations, the family business went from strength to strength throughout the 19th century under the commercial name of Pernod Fils, though the banking family Veil-Picard gradually took over the operation during the 1890s. By 1900 the company was producing 30,000 litres every day in a well-lit and ventilated factory, with exports all over the world including the USA, where absinthe was especially popular in New Orleans, San Francisco, Chicago, and New York.

So how did this popularity arise? As had happened with hashish, it was the French army overseas that acquired the absinthe habit. During the various insurrections in North Africa, and especially while on duty in Algeria, the army was issued with absinthe as a vermifuge and the soldiers subsequently took their new habit back with them to France. Wormwood plants were grown primarily in the valley of the river Doubs, but also in the Jura. The anise came from as far away as the Tarn region and the fennel from the Gard. The macerated plants were initially steeped in brandy prior to distillation, then the colour was adjusted through the addition of extracts of wormwood and hyssop to produce what was described as a *liquor vert olive transparent*.

The absinthe of the 19th century was a very strongly alcoholic product (120-150 proof, 60-75% alcohol by volume). Preparation of an absinthe was quite a work of art, and involved the slow addition of ice-cold water through a perforated spoon bearing a lump of sugar into a glass containing about 30-40 ml of the liquor. The resultant greenish, opalescent solution was not only the drink of soldiers and peasants but the favoured drink of the artists and writers who placed it centrally in their paintings or wrote of its virtues and dangers.

Of this group, perhaps the most infamous was Paul Marie Verlaine. It was Verlaine more than anyone else who inspired the cult surrounding absinthe. Born in 1844, he was a wild youth who began drinking absinthe to excess in his early teens and had numerous early sexual encounters with both prostitutes and other men. Despite these excesses, he published his first book of poems, *Poèmes Saturniens*, in 1866. Soon afterwards he became infatuated with the 17-year-old Mathilde Mauté, marrying her in 1870, but their marital relations were disturbed two years later after he received letters and poems from the young poet Arthur Rimbaud. Verlaine immediately invited Rimbaud to Paris with the words 'come, dear great soul, we summon you, we await you'.

Rimbaud was born in 1854 to a mother who forced on him a serious study of the bible and Latin poetry from an early age. Perhaps as a result of this, he became an extremely gifted pupil at school and won numerous prizes before he too went off the rails as a teenager, turning to drink and petty crime. None the less he produced most of his best poetry between the ages of 16 and 21. He was already something of a rebel by the time he met Verlaine (10 years his senior), and they began a tempestuous two-year affair, fuelled by absinthe and hashish.

During this period Verlaine began abusing Mathilde, including (it is claimed) setting fire to her hair and clothes on one occasion, and submitting her to savage beatings. Rimbaud seems to have encouraged this abuse, declaring that to be a good family man was absurd. In 1872, Rimbaud and Verlaine travelled to England, but their stay was brief and impecunious. In 1873, tiring of their relationship, Rimbaud initiated a break-up, causing a devastated Verlaine to leave for Brussels. He then contacted Rimbaud to announce that he was about to commit suicide, and Rimbaud immediately followed him to Brussels to plead with him. They met, but Verlaine, completely out of his mind with drink, shot his ex-lover in the wrist. This was all too much for the local police, and in light of Verlaine's well-known reputation as a debaucher and drunk he was sentenced to five years in jail.

On his release two years later (he received remission for good behaviour) Verlaine worked for a while as a schoolteacher in England, and appeared to have given up his alcoholic excesses. After he returned to Paris in 1877 he resumed his debauched lifestyle, but in spite of this, he became something of a celebrity in the cafés and bistros of Paris, celebrated as one of the finest *fin de siècle* French poets – the so-called 'decadents' - and even received the title 'Prince of Poets' in 1894. He died aged 51 in 1896, his end hastened by a combination of cirrhosis of the liver and venereal disease. Although a lifelong user of his 'humble ephemeral absinthe', he claimed that opium and hashish were poisons.

Freed from the clutches of Verlaine, Rimbaud produced some excellent prose works during the period 1873-5, as well as a collection of poems under the title *Illuminations*, but then he abandoned writing. For a time he became something of a world traveller and even participated in the slave trade and gun-running in Abyssinia, though he ultimately returned to Marseille suffering from what he believed to be arthritis in his knee. This unfortunately turned out to be a leg cancer and he died from the cancer in 1891 aged just 37 years.

Another inveterate absinthe drinker was the English poet Ernest Dowson. His prose poem *Absinthia Taetra* describes rather well the experience of this liquor that hastened his premature death.

The man let the water trickle gently into his glass, and as the green clouded, a mist fell away from his mind. Then he drank opaline. Green changed to white, emerald to opal... and that obscure night of the soul, and the valley of humiliation, through which he stumbled, were forgotten. He saw blue vistas of undiscovered countries, high prospects and a quiet caressing sea. The past shed its perfume over him... He drank opaline.

At the end of his short life Dowson seems to have revised his opinion of absinthe, declaring 'On the whole it is a mistake to get binged on the verdant fluid. As a steady drink it is inferior to the homely scotch'.

For a brief six-week period in 1897 Dowson shared a close friendship with Oscar Wilde after the latter was released from Reading Jail. Wilde travelled to France but was ostracized by most of the artists and writers, though he was eventually befriended by Dowson when they were both staying near Dieppe. Wilde appears to have had a crush on Dowson, but the latter was not interested in romance, and is even alleged to have persuaded Wilde to partake of the pleasures available in a local brothel. On his emergence Wilde is reputed to have said:

The first in these ten years, and it will be the last. It was like cold mutton. But tell it in England, for it will entirely restore my character.

Some idea of the warmth of this brief friendship can be found in Wilde's letters to Dowson, in one of which he reports 'I decided this morning to take a 'Pernod'. The result was marvellous. At 8.30 I was dead. Now I am alive, and all is perfect except for your absence'.

But neither of them was destined to rekindle this friendship. Wilde is believed to have died from meningitis arising from an ear abscess in November 1900, shortly after the death of his friend in February of the same year aged 32 years.

In addition to these poets, it was the artists of the late nineteenth century who have immortalised absinthe in their paintings. Probably the most famous of these is *the Absinthe Drinker* by Edouard Manet, which was presented for exhibition in the Paris Salon in 1859. It was rejected on the grounds that it depicted an unsavoury character in the shape of an impoverished sifter of city rubbish – an inebriated ragpicker. It would perhaps have been more acceptable to have a professional model dressed as a ragpicker.

Certainly Manet mixed with disreputable characters, being a friend of Charles Baudelaire (of opium fame) from about 1858, and was probably influenced by Baudelaire's alcohol and drug-saturated lifestyle. The latter famously claimed:

One must be drunk always... If you would not feel the burden of time that breaks your shoulders and bows you to the earth, you must intoxicate yourself increasingly.

Manet made several sketches of Baudelaire, and some have compared these likeness with that of the famous ragpicker.

Edgar Degas also produced a painting which attracted much controversy and also distaste. In his famous *l'Absinthe* he depicted the actress Ellen Andrée, who apparently rarely touched alcohol, and also the engraver Marcellin Desboutin, who was also very respectable. The picture, painted in 1876, does depict brilliantly *l'heure d'absinthe* when everything stopped for what Baudelaire termed 'the liquor that contains neither vitality nor death, neither excitation nor extinction'. The painting was severely criticised when first exhibited in Paris under the title *Au Café*. In the same year it appeared in an exhibition in Brighton, and one of the local newspaper critics described the two subjects as 'a brutal sensual-looking French workman and a sickly-looking 'grisette" (a shop girl of easy virtue). When the picture was exhibited (now under the title *L'Absinthe*) in London in 1893 as part of a display of contemporary artists, it attracted particular opprobrium from critics who believed that it was an advertisement for temperance, while others saw it as yet another example of French decadence.

This French decadence and the excitement of the Montmartre district of Paris were probably best depicted by Toulouse-Lautrec. His contemporary, the painter Gustave Moreau, said that 'his paintings were entirely painted in absinthe', and some of his depictions of the brothels and dance halls of Paris do have an hallucinatory glow. Absinthe appeared in many of Toulouse-Lautrec's paintings and he was himself an inveterate absinthist and general alcoholic whose early death in 1901 (aged 36) was not unexpected. He left behind a unique record of the bars, brothels and theatres of Paris in the late 19th century, and probably also introduced that other hallucinatory painter Vincent van Gogh to the pleasures of brothels and absinthe.

Numerous theories have been considered for van Gogh's preference for yellow in his paintings and their overall psychedelic appearance, ranging from the credible effects of glaucoma to his suspected mania, but an over-indulgence in absinthe may also have been contributory. Fearing that his decadent lifestyle in Paris was affecting his artistic output, van Gogh fled to Arles in 1888 (apparently on Lautrec's advice) and subsequently produced some of his best work.

Paul Gauguin arrived in the summer of that year and for a while shared a house with van Gogh. They both frequented the Café de l'Alcazar, which was a popular haunt of alcoholics and degenerates, and van Gogh's absinthe drinking seems to have increased. On Christmas Eve 1888, in an event reminiscent of what passed between

Verlaine and Rimbaud, Van Gogh is said to have feigned an attack on Gauguin with a razor before returning to their house and cutting off his own ear lobe with the same razor. Recently there have been suggestions that Gauguin may have inflicted the wound. This behaviour led to several incarcerations in the local asylum, though he made apparent recoveries and painted some more masterpieces.

Van Gogh's eventual decline began when he added turpentine consumption to his daily round of absinthe drinking. Though he was treated in the asylum at Saint Rémy de Provence from May 1889 to July 1890, his mental state deteriorated. He shot himself in the chest on July 27th and died two days later, aged thirty-seven. While it is generally accepted that there was a family history of mental illness and that Van Gogh was suffering from syphilis at the time of his death, there is little doubt that this was another premature death that has to be blamed at least partly on absinthe.

In contrast to these other artists, Pablo Picasso is not known to have been a great drinker of absinthe, but he did produce a number of paintings and a sculpture (*the Glass of Absinthe*) in 1914, with absinthe as their subject. He, of course, lived a long and very varied life, providing good evidence that absinthe was best left as the subject of artistic output and not consumed.

In his early years Picasso had been somewhat influenced by the drinking habits of the playwright and novelist Alfred Jarry, who in turn had modelled himself on Rimbaud. Jarry came to Paris in 1891 when he was seventeen and set about ruining his health with drink. He was a lifelong misogynist and probably homophilic rather than homosexual, and he apparently drank everything. His supposed only lady friend, the novelist Rachilde (a pen name), wrote that Jarry's daily consumption included as much as two litres of white wine with breakfast followed by two to three absinthes (he took it neat!) mid-morning, with more wine and absinthe with lunch, and a couple of bottles of wine with his dinner.

In his writing Jarry gives the impression that he believed absinthe had the power to enable introspection. He wrote a number of plays, but died aged 34 from the effects of TB and alcoholism. In fact the fate of most of these literary and artistic characters was determined by a combination of their unhealthy lifestyles coupled with their alcoholic intake, and in most instances a large proportion of this alcohol was taken in the form of the 'green fairy'.

Fiction writers also described the use of absinthe in their books; Emile Zola's Nana is one of the best known fictional characters who enjoyed all the excesses of Montmartre. She and her friend Satin would confide in one another about their conquests and other experiences and 'sometimes on afternoons when they were both in the dumps, they would treat themselves to an absinthe to help them forget the beastliness of men'.

The detrimental effects to health of excessive absinthe consumption soon attracted the attentions of the medical fraternity, and a Dr Motet was one of the first to describe the pallid, weak and enfeebled creatures who populated the Parisian Psychiatric Hospital Bicêtre. His report, entitled *Considérations générals sur l'alcoolisme et plus particulièrement des effets toxiques produits sur l'homme par la liqueur d'absinthe*, appeared in 1859. But is was Dr Valentin Magnan who claimed in 1869 to have demonstrated the toxic effects of wormwood, and by implication the major chemical constituent thujone. In the description of his experiment he reported that a guinea pig in a glass cage with a saucer of wormwood extract, and another with a saucer of alcohol, were left to inhale the vapours. The former, after initial excitement, suffered convulsions, while the latter became intoxicated. He also described similar experiments with a cat and a rabbit. Dogs were given large oral doses of absinthe and then suffered epileptic-type seizures, while alcohol simply caused intoxication. This led him to propose that thujone was the culprit, though he did not exclude the possibility that constituents of hyssop and anise might be contributory.

The absinthe industry responded by producing the liquor without thujone (*sans thujone*), but these apparent risks seem to have provided little discouragement for the populace; by 1910 the French were consuming more than 35 million litres each year.

Increasingly governments became alarmed at the rise of alcoholism, especially when it involved absinthe drinking, and its association with criminal behaviour. In Switzerland absinthe was banned in 1910 following a well-publicised murder case involving a vineyard worker called Jean Lanfray. By all accounts Lanfray consumed alcohol in prodigious quantities. On the day in August 1905 when he shot and killed his wife and two young daughters he had consumed several brandies, at least a couple of bottles of wine, and two large glasses of absinthe. The effects and dangers of this last drink attracted most of the press coverage during the trial in 1906. Some of the lawyers and journalists supported the manufacturers in their claims that absinthe was being unduly blamed for the actions of a very obvious general alcoholic, but despite this support, a move to pass laws banning absinthe production moved inexorably through the Swiss parliamentary system.

The temperance movement in France became an increasingly dynamic force. It published statistics showing that the number of people in asylums had increased from around 50,000 in the 1870s to more than 100,000 in the early 1900s, with the majority of these having alcohol (absinthe) related problems. In 1888 the French *Ligue National Contre l'Alcoolisme* obtained 400,000 signatures for a petition declaring that absinthe provoked criminal activities and epilepsy and was ruinous for family life. They also produced some verse that supported their claims:

Je suis la Fée Verte (I am the Green Fairy)
Ma robe est le couleur d'espérance (My dress is the colour of hope)
Je suis la ruine et la douleur (I am ruin and despair)
Je suis la honte (I am disgrace)
Je suis le déshonneur (I am dishonour)
Je suis la mort (I am death)
Je suis l'Absinthe (I am absinthe).

Debate raged in the French National Assembly for many years, and not surprisingly the absinthe producers mounted a vigorous lobby stressing the value to the exchequer of the taxes raised through the sale of absinthe. These exceeded 50 million francs a year by 1910, and this argument was successful right up until the start of the First World War. Now the generals raised objections to the sale of absinthe claiming that they needed sober troops to fight the enemy, and the French Government was forced to enact a law in March 1915 to close down the factories, with essentially no compensation paid to the manufacturers. The tide had already turned against absinthe, partly because of a spate of grisly murders perpetrated by alleged *absinthists*, but also because there were growing fears about the declining birth rate in France, which was blamed upon the supposed sterilising effects of absinthe.

France was the last major country to ban absinthe, since the USA had introduced a ban in 1912. There was no reason for a ban in the UK because absinthe drinking had not been a problem. Spain also allowed production of absinthe to continue and Pernod moved their production to Catalonia, while maintaining anise-based liquor production in France in the form of their product pastis. Interestingly, since about 2000, many countries, including France, have allowed a revival of absinthe production and sale, and this followed an evaluation of the toxicological properties of thujone by a WHO commission entitled *Codex Alimentarius* in 1979. This commission recommended that thujone could be used as a flavouring (bittering) material provided that its concentration did not exceed 10mg of thujone per kg of alcoholic beverage (25% maximum volume of alcohol), and more recently this has been amended to 35mg/kg. The USA has thus far refused to accept these recommendations, and the maximum amount of thujone allowed in any alcoholic beverage is 10mg/litre of beverage. The upshot of these recommendations is the appearance of a plethora of new products with names like Moulin Rooz and la Fée Absinthe – names that are calculated to revive and extend the cult status of the liquor.

Can we separate myth from reality, or the genuine alcoholic from the more ephemeral absinthist? The dogma originally established by Dr Magnan was that thujone was the toxic ingredient which led to the state of absinthism. In his earliest publication in 1864 for *l'Union Médicale* under the title *Accidents déterminés par la liqueur d'absinthe* he reported a study of a patient who regularly drank five to six glasses of absinthe each day together with quantities of wine and *eau de vie*. This man entered the hospital on several occasions with what Magnan described as *delirium tremens*, though he seemed to progress to a state where he suffered extreme hallucinations and epileptic seizures. Magnan summarised his case and blamed these later manifestations on absinthe.

As mentioned earlier, his comparative experiments on animals seemed to confirm that absinthe rather than alcohol per se could induce epileptic seizures, though he did administer gram quantities of the liquor, either mixed in with bread or directly into the veins of the animals.

There was considerable controversy over the next 25 years, and contradictory results were obtained by two very brave physiologists (Cadéac and Meunier) from Lyon who self-administered a gram of what was described as *essence of absinthe* and reported a stimulant effect. They calculated that they had consumed the equivalent of 60-200 glasses of absinthe in this experiment. Not withstanding these and other apparently contradictory findings, Magnan waged an incessant war against alcoholism and what he believed to be the associated condition of absinthism.

Certainly thujone is known to possess activity in the brain and can lead to epileptic-like seizures at a dose of several hundred milligrams. Over the years various claims have been made for thujone levels in absinthe as high as 260mg per litre, which would mean around 9mg of thujone in a typical 35ml glass of neat absinthe. However, a definitive and fascinating study was carried out by the German group Lachenmeier in 2007 (reported in 2008) on 13 bottles of pre-ban (ie pre 1915) absinthe, which revealed typical thujone contents of 0.5 to 48mg/litre with a mean value of 33mg/litre. These vintage bottles of absinthe were sourced from as far back as 1895 from Edouard Pernod of Switzerland and Pernod Fils of France. They also analysed some post-ban absinthe (mainly from Spain), including some illicit absinthe from Val de Travers in Switzerland, and none of these contained more than 33mg per litre.

Two features of their analytical results are particularly noteworthy: the variability of the thujone levels and the quite large amounts of another chemical substance, fenchone (up to 45mg/litre) that were also present. Neither of these findings is surprising, since the fenchone comes from hyssop, and any herbal extract will vary in its composition depending on the source of the plant and the time of harvesting. This is the perennial problem with herbal medicines where the consumer has no way of assessing the variability of the preparations and consequently their likely efficacy. What is clear is that there was no sign of the large amounts of thujone claimed for 19th century absinthe, although the long-term harmful effects of say 9mg of thujone per glass should not be underestimated. However, compared with the vast amounts of ethanol that were being consumed contemporaneously, the amounts of thujone pale into insignificance.

Of course this all rather spoils the story, since it is likely that Dowson, Rimbaud, Verlaine, and all the other absinthists were in reality nothing more than hardened alcoholics, and that the exciting mental effects claimed for *la Fée Verte* were little more than those associated with intoxication. Not that these revelations and consequent reality check will do anything to dampen the enthusiasm for the cult of absinthe. Five minutes spent on the Internet reveals a veritable bazaar of absinthe-related products and publications.

This book began with an account of LSD, probably the most potent hallucinogen ever encountered by human cultures, and ends with a putative euphoriant which was something of a damp squib. The one feature that these two products, and all of the other substances mentioned in this book share, is the colourful characters who have popularised their use. These people and the drugs they have used and abused have had a huge impact on history, politics, social structure, and culture. The individual psychedelics, narcotics and euphoriants are all now illegal or tightly controlled, so recreational use is fraught with danger. However, the potential medical use of these substances is only now being explored. LSD looks to be promising as a drug to reduce the anxiety and pain of terminal cancer, while the THC-containing drug Sativex is effective for relieving some of the symptoms of multiple sclerosis. Perhaps most surprising, ecstasy can help patients with post traumatic stress disorder. It is not impossible that in the future an alternative form of Timothy Leary's slogan might read 'turn on, tune in and feel the medicinal benefit'.

ND - #0504 - 270225 - C0 - 234/156/14 - PB - 9781909020382 - Matt Lamination